S0-BHR-925

YOUR PERSONAL
HOROSCOPE
2015

TAURUS

YOUR PERSONAL HOROSCOPE 2015

TAURUS

21st April–21st May

igloobooks

igloobooks

Published in 2014
by Igloo Books Ltd

Cottage Farm
Sywell
NN6 0BJ
www.igloobooks.com

Copyright © 2014 W. Foulsham & Co. Ltd

Produced for Igloo Books by W. Foulsham & Co. Ltd, The Old Barrel Store,
Drayman's Lane, Marlow, Bucks SL7 2FF, England

The Copyright Act prohibits (subject to certain very limited exceptions) the making of copies of
any copyright work or of a substantial part of such a work, including the making of copies by
photocopying or similar process. Written permission to make a copy or copies must therefore
normally be obtained from the publisher in advance. It is advisable also to consult the publisher if
in any doubt as to the legality of any copying which is to be undertaken.

HUN001 0714
2 4 6 8 10 9 7 5 3 1
ISBN: 978-1-783-43647-7

This is an abridged version of material originally published
in Old Moore's Horoscope and Astral Diary.

Printed and manufactured in China

CONTENTS

CONTENTS

INTRODUCTION

Your Personal Horoscopes have been specifically created to allow you to get the most from astrological patterns and the way they have a bearing on not only your zodiac sign, but nuances within it. Using the diary section of the book you can read about the influences and possibilities of each and every day of the year. It will be possible for you to see when you are likely to be cheerful and happy or those times when your nature is in retreat and you will be more circumspect. The diary will help to give you a feel for the specific 'cycles' of astrology and the way they can subtly change your day-to-day life. For example, when you see the sign ☿, this means that the planet Mercury is retrograde at that time. Retrograde means it appears to be running backwards through the zodiac. Such a happening has a significant effect on communication skills, but this is only one small aspect of how the Personal Horoscope can help you.

With Your Personal Horoscope the story doesn't end with the diary pages. It includes simple ways for you to work out the zodiac sign the Moon occupied at the time of your birth, and what this means for your personality. In addition, if you know the time of day you were born, it is possible to discover your Ascendant, yet another important guide to your personal make-up and potential.

Many readers are interested in relationships and in knowing how well they get on with people of other astrological signs. You might also be interested in the way you appear to very different sorts of individuals. If you are such a person, the section on Venus will be of particular interest. Despite the rapidly changing position of this planet, you can work out your Venus sign, and learn what bearing it will have on your life.

Using Your Personal Horoscope you can travel on one of the most fascinating and rewarding journeys that anyone can take – the journey to a better realisation of self.

INTRODUCTION

THE ESSENCE OF TAURUS

Exploring the Personality of Taurus the Bull

(21ST APRIL – 21ST MAY)

What's in a sign?

Taurus is probably one of the most misunderstood signs of the zodiac. Astrologers from the past described those born under the sign of the Bull as being gentle, artistic, stubborn and refined. All of this is quite true, but there is so much more to Taureans and the only reason it isn't always discussed as much as it should be is because of basic Taurean reserve. Taureans are generally modest, and don't tend to assert themselves in a direct sense, unless in self-defence. As a result the sign is often sidelined, if not ignored.

You know what you want from life and are quite willing to work long and hard to get it. However, Taurus is also a great lover of luxury, so when circumstances permit you can be slow, ponderous and even lax. If there is a paradox here it is merely typical of Venus-ruled Taurus. On differing occasions you can be chatty or quiet, bold or timorous, smart or scruffy. It all depends on your commitment to a situation. When you are inspired there is nobody powerful enough to hold you back and when you are passionate you have the proclivities of a Casanova!

There are aspects of your nature that seldom change. For example, you are almost always friendly and approachable, and invariably have a sense of what feels and looks just right. You are capable and can work with your hands as well as your brain. You don't particularly care for dirt or squalid surroundings, preferring cleanliness, and you certainly don't take kindly to abject poverty. Most Taureans prefer the country to the coast, find loving relationships easy to deal with and are quite committed to home and family.

Whilst variety is the spice of life to many zodiac signs this is not necessarily the case for Taurus. Many people born under the sign of the Bull remain happy to occupy a specific position for years on end. It has been suggested, with more than a grain of truth, that the only thing that can get the Bull moving on occasions is a strategically placed bomb. What matters most, and which shows regularly in your dealings with the world at large, is your innate kindness and your desire to help others.

Taurus resources

The best word to describe Taurean subjects who are working to the best of their ability would be 'practical'. Nebulous situations, where you have to spend long hours thinking things through in a subconscious manner, don't suit you half as much as practical tasks, no matter how complex these might be. If you were to find yourself cast up on a desert island you would have all the necessities of life sorted out in a flash. This is not to suggest that you always recognise this potential in yourself. The problem here is that a very definite lack of self-belief is inclined to make you think that almost anyone else in the world has the edge when it comes to talent.

Another of your greatest resources is your creative potential. You always have the knack of knowing what looks and feels just right. This is as true when it comes to decorating your home as it is regarding matters out there in the big, wide world. If this skill could be allied to confidence on a regular basis, there would be little or nothing to stop you. You may well possess specific skills which others definitely don't have, and you get on best when these are really needed.

Taureans don't mind dealing with routine matters and you have a good administrative ability in a number of different fields. With a deeply intuitive streak (when you are willing to recognise it), it isn't usually hard for you to work out how any particular individual would react under given circumstances. Where you fall down on occasions is that you don't always recognise the great advantages that are yours for the taking, and self-belief could hardly be considered the Taurean's greatest virtue.

Taurus people are good at making lists, even if these are of the mental variety. Your natural warmth makes it possible for you to find friends where others would not, and the sort of advice that you offer is considered and sensible. People feel they can rely on you, a fact that could prove to be one of the most important of your resources. There is nothing at all wrong with using this ability to feather your own nest, particularly since you are not the sort of person who would willingly stand on those around you in order to get where you want to go.

Beneath the surface

To say that you are deep would be a definite understatement. Only you know how far down into the basement some of your considerations and emotions actually go. Because you exhibit a generally practical face to the world at large the true scope of the Taurean mind remains something of a mystery to those around you. Certainly you seem to be uncomplicated and even a little superficial at times, though nothing could be further from the truth. Very little happens to you that fails to be filed away in some recess or other of that great interior that is your mind's library. It may be because of this that Taurus is well known for being able to bear a grudge for a long time. However, what is sometimes forgotten is that you never let a kindness from someone else go without reward, even though it may take you a very long time to find a way to say thank you.

Affairs of the heart are of special importance to you and ties of the romantic kind go as deep as any emotion. Once you love you tend to do so quite unconditionally. It takes months or years of upsets to shake your faith in love, and it's a fact that even in these days of marital splits, Taureans are far more likely than most signs of the zodiac to remain hitched. The simple fact is that you believe in loyalty, absolutely and irrevocably. The thought of letting anyone down once you have given your word is almost unthinkable and if such a situation does occur there are almost always quite definite mitigating factors.

Rules and regulations are easy for you to deal with because you have a natural tendency to order. You are also fairly good at dealing with routines and probably have your own life well sorted out as a result. A word of caution is necessary only when this internal need for order extends too much into your external life. Taureans can be fanatical about having a tidy house or for making things work out exactly as they would wish in a work sense. These tendencies start within the recesses of your own, often closed, mind. The way forward here is to throw open the doors and windows now and again and to let those around you know how you function internally. It isn't easy, because you are quite a closed book at heart. However the exercise is well worthwhile and the results can be quite breathtaking.

Making the best of yourself

Anyone who wants to work to the best of their ability first needs a good deal of self-knowledge. In your case this means recognising just what you are capable of doing and then concentrating in these directions. Of course it's only human nature to be all the things we are not, but this tendency runs deeper in you than it does in the majority of individuals. Use your natural kindness to the full and ally this to your practical ability to get things done. Sorting things out is easy for you, so easy in fact that you sometimes fail to realise that not everyone has these skills to the same extent.

Confidence definitely seems to be evident in the way you deal with the world at large. Of course you know that this often isn't the case, but that doesn't matter. It's the way the world at large views you that counts, so keep moving forward, even on those occasions when you are shaking inside. Use your naturally creative skills to the full and cultivate that innate sense of order in ways that benefit you and the world at a very practical level.

Avoid the tendency to be stubborn by convincing yourself that so many things 'simply don't matter'. An inability to move, simply because you feel annoyed or aggrieved, is certainly going to be more of a hindrance than a help – though there are occasions when, like all facets of nature, it's essential. Cultivate the more cheerful qualities that are endemic to your nature and be prepared to mix freely with as many different sorts of people as you possibly can. Be willing to take on new responsibilities because the more you are able to do so, the greater is your natural sense of self-worth. Stitching all these qualities together and using them to your own advantage isn't always easy, but pays handsomely in the end.

The impressions you give

This is a very interesting section as far as the sign of Taurus is concerned. The reason is very simply that you fail on so many occasions to betray the sheer depth of your own Earth-sign nature. That doesn't mean to say that you come across badly to others. On the contrary, you are probably a very popular person, except with those people who mistreat or cheat others. You have a great sense of what is right, and don't tend to deviate from a point of view once you've come to terms with it.

The world sees you as capable, cheerful and generally active, though with a tendency to be sluggish and lethargic on occasions. Perhaps Taurus needs to explain itself more because even when you are not at your most vibrant best there are invariably reasons. You can be quite secretive, though only usually about yourself. This can make life with the Taurean something of a guessing game on occasions. Certainly you appear to be much more fixed in your attitude than might often be the case. Why should this be so? It's mainly because you do have extremely definite ideas about specific matters, and since you sometimes display these it's natural that others pigeon-hole you as a very 'definite' sort. Actually this is far from being the whole truth but, once again, if you don't explain yourself, others can be left in the dark.

You almost certainly are not short of friends. People recognise that you are friendly, tolerant and extremely supportive. You give the impression of being very trustworthy and people know that they can rely on you to act in a specific manner. If this appears to make you somewhat predictable it doesn't really matter because you are deeply loved, and that's what counts. One fact is almost certain – the world has a greater regard for you in a general sense than you have for yourself.

13

The way forward

The ideal life for the Taurus subject seems to be one that is settled and happy, with not too much upheaval and plenty of order. Whether or not this truly turns out to be the case depends on a number of factors. For starters, even those born under the sign of the Bull have a boredom threshold. This means that having to respond to change and diversity probably does you more good than you might at first think. At the same time you won't know exactly what you are capable of doing unless you really stretch yourself, and that's something that you are not always willing to do.

You do function best from within loving relationships, and although you can be very passionate, once you have given your heart you don't tend to change your mind readily. Personal and domestic contentment are worth a great deal to you because they represent the platform upon which you build the rest of your life. You don't make a good itinerant and probably won't indulge in travel for its own sake. Of course it does you good to get around, since anything that broadens your horizons has got to be an advantage, but you'll probably always maintain a solid home base and relish the prospect of coming back to it as frequently as possible.

Most Taureans are family people. You can be a capable parent, though tend to be a little more authoritarian than some types. Keeping an ordered sort of life is at the base of your psychology, so that even when you are young and less tidy-minded there is always a basic desire for self-discipline. This often extends to your work, where you are extremely capable and can quite easily work under your own supervision. You recognise the beautiful in all spheres of life and tend to gravitate towards clean and sanitary surroundings.

In matters of health you tend to be fairly robust, though you can suffer somewhat with headaches, often brought about as a result of a stiff neck and stress. This latter is what you should avoid as much as possible. Saying what you feel, and listening carefully to the responses, is definitely of great importance. The more you learn, the wiser you become. This makes you the natural resort of others when they need help and advice. If you try not to underestimate your own abilities, you can rise as far in life as the world at large thinks you are capable of doing. At the end of the day it is important to recognise your popularity. In all probability your friends have a much higher opinion of you than the one you cultivate for yourself.

TAURUS ON THE CUSP

Astrological profiles are altered for those people born at either the beginning or the end of a zodiac sign, or, more properly, on the cusps of a sign. In the case of Taurus this would be on the 21st of April and for two or three days after, and similarly at the end of the sign, probably from the 18th to the 21st of May.

The Aries Cusp – April 21st to April 24th

Although you have all the refinement, breeding and creative flair of the true Taurean, you are definitely more of a go-getter. Knowing what you want from life there is a slight possibility that you might be accused of being bossy and sometimes this slightly hurts your Taurean sensitivity. You have plenty of energy to get through the things that you see as being important but it is quite possible that those around you don't always see things in the same light, and this can be annoying to you. Like the typical Taurean you have great reserves of energy and can work long and hard towards any particular objective although, because Aries is also in attendance, you may push yourself slightly harder than is strictly necessary. Your temper is variable and you may not always display the typical Taurean patience with those around you.

It is possible for Taurus to 'wait in the wings' deliberately and therefore to lose out on some of the most important potential gains as a result. In your case, this is much less likely. You don't worry too much about speaking your mind. You are loving and kind, but even family members know that they will only be able to push you so far. At work, you are capable and have executive ability. Like the Taurean you don't really care for getting your hands dirty, but if needs must you can pitch in with the best of them and enjoy a challenge. You don't worry as much as some of your Taurean friends do, but all the same you regularly expect too much of your nervous system and need frequent periods of rest.

Try not to impose your will on those around you and be content to allow things to happen on their own sometimes. This might not be an easy thing for the Aries-cusp Taurean but it's one of the sure ways to success. Confidence isn't lacking and neither is basic patience, but they do have to be encouraged and nurtured.

The Gemini Cusp – May 18th to May 21st

Oh, what a happy person you are – and how much the world loves you for it! This is definitely the more potentially fortunate of the two Taurean cusps, or at least that is how the majority of the people who know you would view it. The fact is that you are bright and breezy, easygoing and sometimes fickle on occasions, but supporting these trends is a patient, generally contented attitude to life that is both refreshing and inspiring. Getting others on your side is not hard and you have plenty of energy when it is needed the most. All the same you are quite capable of dozing in the sun occasionally and probably put far less stress on your nervous system than either Taurus or Gemini when taken alone.

You don't care too much for routines and you love variety, but yet you retain the creative and artistic qualities that come with the sign of the Bull. You work well and with confidence, but would be very likely to change direction in your career at some stage in your life and are not half so tied to routine as is usually the case for Taurus. With a friendly, and even a passionate, approach to matters of the heart you are an attentive lover and a fond parent. Most people know what you really are because you are only too willing to show them. Working out the true motivations that lurk within your soul is part of your personal search to know 'self' and is extremely important.

All in all, you have exactly what it takes to get on in life and a sense of joy and fun that makes you good to know. Patience balances your need to 'get going', whilst your mischievous streak lightens the load of the sign of Taurus which can, on occasions, take itself rather more seriously than it should.

There are many ways of coping with the requirements of life and, at one time or another, it is likely that you will try them all out. But above and beyond your need to experiment you know what is most important to you and that will always be your ultimate goal. What matters the most is your smile, which is enduring and even alluring.

TAURUS AND ITS ASCENDANTS

The nature of every individual on the planet is composed of the rich variety of zodiac signs and planetary positions that were present at the time of their birth. Your Sun sign, which in your case is Taurus, is one of the many factors when it comes to assessing the unique person you are. Probably the most important consideration, other than your Sun sign, is to establish the zodiac sign that was rising over the eastern horizon at the time that you were born. This is your Ascending or Rising sign. Most popular astrology fails to take account of the Ascendant, and yet its importance remains with you from the very moment of your birth, through every day of your life. The Ascendant is evident in the way you approach the world, and so, when meeting a person for the first time, it is this astrological influence that you are most likely to notice first. Our Ascending sign essentially represents what we appear to be, while the Sun sign is what we feel inside ourselves.

The Ascendant also has the potential for modifying our overall nature. For example, if you were born at a time of day when Taurus was passing over the eastern horizon (this would be around the time of dawn) then you would be classed as a double Taurus. As such, you would typify this zodiac sign, both internally and in your dealings with others. However, if your Ascendant sign turned out to be a Fire sign, such as Leo, there would be a profound alteration of nature, away from the expected qualities of Taurus.

One of the reasons why popular astrology often ignores the Ascendant is that it has always been rather difficult to establish. We have found a way to make this possible by devising an easy-to-use table, which you will find on page 157 of this book. Using this, you can establish your Ascendant sign at a glance. You will need to know your rough time of birth, then it is simply a case of following the instructions.

For those readers who have no idea of their time of birth it might be worth allowing a good friend, or perhaps your partner, to read through the section that follows this introduction. Someone who deals with you on a regular basis may easily discover your Ascending sign, even though you could have some difficulty establishing it for yourself. A good understanding of this component of your nature is essential if you want to be aware of that 'other person' who is responsible for the way you make contact with the world at large. Your Sun sign, Ascendant sign, and the other pointers in this book will, together, allow you a far better understanding of what makes you tick as an individual. Peeling back the different layers of your astrological make-up can be an enlightening experience, and the Ascendant may represent one of the most important layers of all.

Taurus with Taurus Ascendant

The world would see you as being fairly typical of the sign of Taurus, so you are careful, sensitive, well bred and, if other astrological trends agree, very creative. Nothing pleases you more than a tidy environment to live in and a peaceful life. You probably believe that there is a place for everything and will do your best to keep it all where it should be. It's a pity that this sometimes includes people, and you are certain to get rather irritated if they don't behave in the way that you would expect. Despite this, you are generally understanding and are very capable of giving and receiving affection.

Not everyone knows the real you, however, and it is sometimes difficult to tell the world those most personal details that can be locked deep inside. At an emotional level you tend to idealise love somewhat, though if anything this presents itself to the world as a slight 'coldness' on occasions. This is far from the truth, but your tidy mind demands that even the most intimate processes are subjected to the same sense of order with which you view the world at large. Unlike many sign combinations, you don't really rely on the help and support of others because you are more than capable yourself. In the main you live a happy life and have the ability to pass on this trait to those you care for.

Taurus with Gemini Ascendant

This is a generally happy combination which finds you better able to externalise the cultured and creative qualities which are inherent in your Taurean nature. You love to be around interesting and stimulating people and tend to be much more talkative than the typical Taurean is expected to be. The reason why Gemini helps here is because it lightens the load somewhat. Taurus is not the most introspective sign of the zodiac, but it does have that quality, and a good dose of Gemini allows you to speak your mind more freely and, as a result, to know yourself better too.

Although your mind tends to be fairly logical, you also enjoy flashes of insight that can cause you to behave in a less rational way from time to time. This is probably no bad thing because life will never be boring with you around. You try to convince yourself that you take on board all the many and varied opinions that come back at you from others, though there is a slight danger of intellectual snobbery if the responses you get are not the expected ones. You particularly like clean houses, funny people and probably fast cars. Financial rewards can come thick and fast to the Gemini-Ascendant Taurean when the logical but inspirational mind is harnessed to practical matters.

Taurus with Cancer Ascendant

Your main aim in life seems to be to look after everyone and everything that you come across. From your deepest and most enduring human love, right down to the birds in the park, you really do care and you show that natural affection in a thousand different ways. Your nature is sensitive and you are easily moved to tears, though this does not prevent you from pitching in and doing practical things to assist at just about any level. There is a danger that you could stifle those same people whom you set out to assist, and people with this zodiac combination are often unwilling, or unable, to allow their children to grow and leave the nest. More time spent considering what suits you would be no bad thing, but the problem is that you find it almost impossible to imagine any situation that doesn't involve your most basic need, which is to nurture.

You appear not to possess a selfish streak, though it sometimes turns out that, in being certain that you understand the needs and wants of the world, you are nevertheless treading on their toes. This eventual realisation can be very painful, but it isn't a stick with which you should beat yourself because at heart you are one of the kindest people imaginable. Your sense of fair play means that you are a quiet social reformer at heart.

Taurus with Leo Ascendant

Oh dear, this can be rather a hedonistic combination. The trouble is that Taurus tends to have a great sense of what looks and feels right, whilst Leo, being a Cat, is inclined to preen itself on almost any occasion. The combination tends towards self-love, which is all too likely for someone who is perfect. But don't be too dispirited about these facts because there is a great deal going for you in other ways. For a start you have one of the warmest hearts to be found anywhere and you are so brave that others marvel at the courage you display. The mountains that you climb may not be of the large, rocky sort, but you manage to find plenty of pinnacles to scale all the same, and you invariably get to the top.

Routines might bore you a little more than would be the case with Taurus alone, but you don't mind being alone. Why should you? You are probably the nicest person you know! Thus if you were ever to be cast up on a deserted island you would people the place all on your own, and there would never be any crime, untidiness or arguments. Problems only arise when other people are involved. However, in social settings you are charming, good to know and full of ideas that really have legs. You preserve your youth well into middle age, but at base you can tend to worry more than is good for you.

Taurus with Virgo Ascendant

This combination tends to amplify the Taurean qualities that you naturally possess and this is the case because both Taurus and Virgo are Earth signs. However, there are certain factors related to Virgo that show themselves very differently than the sign's cousin Taurus. Virgo is more fussy, nervy and and pedantic than Taurus and all of these qualities are going to show up in your nature at one level or another. On the plus side, you might be slightly less concerned about having a perfect home and a perfect family, and your interest in life appears at a more direct level than that of the true Taurean. You care very much about your home and family and are very loyal to your friends. It's true that you sometimes tend to try and take them over, and you can also show a marked tendency to dominate, but your heart is in the right place, and most people recognise that your caring is genuine.

One problem is that there are very few shades of grey in your life, which is certainly not the case for other zodiac sign combinations. Living your life in the way that you do, there isn't much room for compromise, and this fact alone can prove to be something of a problem where relationships are concerned. In a personal sense you need a partner who is willing to be organised and one who relies heavily on your judgements, which don't change very often.

Taurus with Libra Ascendant

A fortunate combination in many ways, this is a double Venus rulership, since both Taurus and Libra are heavily reliant on the planet of love. You are social, amiable and a natural diplomat, anxious to please and ready to care for just about anyone who shows interest in you. You hate disorder, which means that there is a place for everything and everything in its place. This can throw up the odd paradox, however, since being half Libran you cannot always work out where that place ought to be! You deal with life in a humorous way and are quite capable of seeing the absurd in yourself, as well as in others. Your heart is no bigger than that of the dyed-in-the-wool Taurean, but it sits rather closer to the surface and so others recognise it more.

On those occasions when you know you are standing on firm ground you can show great confidence, even if you have to be ready to change some of your opinions at the drop of a hat. When this happens you can be quite at odds with yourself, because Taurus doesn't take very many U-turns, whereas Libra does. Don't expect to know yourself too well, and keep looking for the funny side of things, because it is within humour that you forge the sort of life that suits you best.

Taurus with Scorpio Ascendant

The first, last and most important piece of advice for you is not to take yourself, or anyone else, too seriously. This might be rather a tall order because Scorpio intensifies the deeper qualities of Taurus and can make you rather lacking in the sense of humour that we all need to live our lives in this most imperfect of worlds. You are naturally sensuous by nature. This shows itself in a host of ways. In all probability you can spend hours in the bath, love to treat yourself to good food and drink and take your greatest pleasure in neat and orderly surroundings. On occasions this can alienate you from those who live in the same house, because other people do need to use the bathroom from time to time, and they cannot remain tidy indefinitely.

You tend to worry a great deal about things which are really not very important, but don't take this statement too seriously or you will begin to worry about this, too! You often need to lighten up and should always do your best to tell yourself that most things are not half so important as they seem to be. Be careful over the selection of a life partner and if possible choose someone who is naturally funny and who does not take life anywhere near as seriously as you are inclined to do. At work you are more than capable and in all probability everyone relies heavily on your wise judgements.

Taurus with Sagittarius Ascendant

A dual nature is evident here, and if it doesn't serve to confuse you, it will certainly be a cause of concern to many of the people with whom you share your life. You like to have a good time and are a natural party-goer. On such occasions you are accommodating, chatty and good to know. But contrast this with the quieter side of Taurus, which is directly opposed to your Sagittarian qualities. The opposition of forces is easy for you to deal with because you inhabit your own body and mind all the time, but it's far less easy for friends and relatives to understand. So on those occasions when you decide that, socially speaking, enough is enough, you may have trouble explaining this to the twelve people who are waiting outside your door with party hats and whoopee cushions.

Confidence to do almost anything is not far from the forefront of your mind and you readily embark on adventures that would have some types flapping about in horror. Here again, it is important to realise that we are not all built the same way and that gentle coaxing is sometimes necessary to bring others round to your point of view. If you really have a fault it could be that you are so busy being your own, rather less than predictable self, that you fail to take the rest of the world into account.

Taurus with Capricorn Ascendant

It might appear on the surface that you are not the most interesting person in the world. This is a pity, for you have an active though very logical mind, so logical in some instances that you would have a great deal in common with Mr Spock. This is the thorn in your flesh, or rather the flesh of everyone else, since you are probably quite happy being exactly what you are. You can think things through in a clear and very practical way and end up taking decisions that are balanced, eminently sensible, but, on occasions, rather dull.

Actually there is a fun machine somewhere deep within that Earth-sign nature and those who know you the best will recognise the fact. Often this combination is attended by a deep and biting sense of humour, but it's of the sort that less intelligent and considered types would find rather difficult to recognise. It is likely that you have no lack of confidence in your own judgement and you have all the attributes necessary to do very well on the financial front. Slow and steady progress is your way and you need to be quite certain before you commit yourself to any new venture. This is a zodiac combination that can soak up years of stress and numerous difficulties, yet still come out on top. Nothing holds you back for long and you tend to be very brave.

Taurus with Aquarius Ascendant

There is nothing that you fail to think about deeply and with great intensity. You are wise, honest and very scientific in your approach to life. Routines are necessary in life, but you have most of them sorted out well in advance and so always have time to look at the next interesting fact. If you don't spend all your time watching documentaries on the television set, you make a good friend and love to socialise. Most of the great discoveries of the world were probably made by people with this sort of astrological combination, though your nature is rather 'odd' on occasions and so can be rather difficult for others to understand.

You may be most surprised when others tell you that you are eccentric, but you don't really mind too much because for half of the time you are not inhabiting the same world as the rest of us. Because you can be delightfully dotty you are probably much loved and cherished by your friends, of which there are likely to be many. Family members probably adore you too and you can be guaranteed to entertain anyone with whom you come into contact. The only fly in the ointment is that you sometimes lose track of reality, whatever that might be, and fly high in your own atmosphere of rarefied possibilities.

Taurus with Pisces Ascendant

You are clearly a very sensitive type of person and that sometimes makes it rather difficult for others to know how they might best approach you. Private and deep, you are nevertheless socially inclined on many occasions. However, because your nature is bottomless it is possible that some types would actually accuse you of being shallow. How can this come about? Well, it's simple really. The fact is that you rarely show anyone what is going on in the deepest recesses of your mind and so your responses can appear to be trite or even ill-considered. This is far from the truth, as those who are allowed into the 'inner sanctum' would readily admit. You are something of a sensualist, and relish staying in bed late and simply pleasing yourself for days on end. However, you are a Taurean at heart so you desire a tidy environment in which to live your usually long life.

You are able to deal with the routine aspects of life quite well and can be a capable worker once you are up and firing on all cylinders. It is very important that you maintain an interest in what you are doing because the recesses of your dreamy mind can sometimes appear to be infinitely more attractive. Your imagination is second to none and this fact can often be turned to your advantage.

Taurus with Aries Ascendant

This is a steady combination, so much so that even experienced astrologers would be unlikely to recognise that the Aries quality is present at all, unless of course they came to know you very well. Your approach to life tends to be slow and considered and there is a great danger that you could suppress those feelings that others of your kind would be only too willing to verbalise. To compensate, you are deeply creative and will think matters through much more readily than more dominant Aries types would be inclined to do. In your dealings with the world, you are, nevertheless, somewhat locked inside yourself and can struggle to achieve the level of communication that you so desperately need. Frustration might follow, were it not for the fact that you possess a quiet determination that, to those in the know, is the clearest window through to your Taurean soul.

The care for others is strong and you certainly demonstrate this at all levels. The fact is that you live a great percentage of your life in service to the people you take to, whilst at the same time being able to shut the door firmly in the face of people who irritate or anger you. You are deeply motivated towards family relationships.

THE MOON AND THE PART IT PLAYS IN YOUR LIFE

In astrology the Moon is probably the single most important heavenly body after the Sun. Its unique position, as partner to the Earth on its journey around the solar system, means that the Moon appears to pass through the signs of the zodiac extremely quickly. The zodiac position of the Moon at the time of your birth plays a great part in personal character and is especially significant in the build-up of your emotional nature.

Your Own Moon Sign

Discovering the position of the Moon at the time of your birth has always been notoriously difficult because tracking the complex zodiac positions of the Moon is not easy. This process has been reduced to three simple stages with our Lunar Tables. A breakdown of the Moon's zodiac positions can be found from page 35 onwards, so that once you know what your Moon Sign is, you can see what part this plays in the overall build-up of your personal character.

If you follow the instructions on the next page you will soon be able to work out exactly what zodiac sign the Moon occupied on the day that you were born and you can then go on to compare the reading for this position with those of your Sun sign and your Ascendant. It is partly the comparison between these three important positions that goes towards making you the unique individual you are.

HOW TO DISCOVER YOUR MOON SIGN

This is a three-stage process. You may need a pen and a piece of paper but if you follow the instructions below the process should only take a minute or so.

STAGE 1 First of all you need to know the Moon Age at the time of your birth. If you look at Moon Table 1, on page 33, you will find all the years between 1917 and 2015 down the left side. Find the year of your birth and then trace across to the right to the month of your birth. Where the two intersect you will find a number. This is the date of the New Moon in the month that you were born. You now need to count forward the number of days between the New Moon and your own birthday. For example, if the New Moon in the month of your birth was shown as being the 6th and you were born on the 20th, your Moon Age Day would be 14. If the New Moon in the month of your birth came after your birthday, you need to count forward from the New Moon in the previous month. Whatever the result, jot this number down so that you do not forget it.

STAGE 2 Take a look at Moon Table 2 on page 34. Down the left hand column look for the date of your birth. Now trace across to the month of your birth. Where the two meet you will find a letter. Copy this letter down alongside your Moon Age Day.

STAGE 3 Moon Table 3 on page 34 will supply you with the zodiac sign the Moon occupied on the day of your birth. Look for your Moon Age Day down the left hand column and then for the letter you found in Stage 2. Where the two converge you will find a zodiac sign and this is the sign occupied by the Moon on the day that you were born.

Your Zodiac Moon Sign Explained

You will find a profile of all zodiac Moon Signs on pages 35 to 38, showing in yet another way how astrology helps to make you into the individual that you are. In each daily entry of the Astral Diary you can find the zodiac position of the Moon for every day of the year. This also allows you to discover your lunar birthdays. Since the Moon passes through all the signs of the zodiac in about a month, you can expect something like twelve lunar birthdays each year. At these times you are likely to be emotionally steady and able to make the sort of decisions that have real, lasting value.

MOON TABLE 1

YEAR	MAR	APR	MAY	YEAR	MAR	APR	MAY	YEAR	MAR	APR	MAY
1917	23	22	20	1950	18	17	17	1983	14	13	12
1918	12	11	10	1951	7	6	6	1984	2	1	1/30
1919	2/31	30	29	1952	25	24	23	1985	21	20	19
1920	20	18	18	1953	15	13	13	1986	10	9	8
1921	9	8	7	1954	5	3	2	1987	29	28	27
1922	28	27	26	1955	24	22	21	1988	18	16	15
1923	17	16	15	1956	12	11	10	1989	7	6	5
1924	5	4	3	1957	1/31	29	29	1990	26	25	24
1925	24	23	22	1958	20	19	18	1991	15	13	13
1926	14	12	11	1959	9	8	7	1992	4	3	2
1927	3	2	1/30	1960	27	26	26	1993	24	22	21
1928	21	20	19	1961	16	15	14	1994	12	11	10
1929	11	9	9	1962	6	5	4	1995	30	29	29
1930	30	28	28	1963	25	23	23	1996	19	18	18
1931	19	18	17	1964	14	12	11	1997	9	7	6
1932	7	6	5	1965	2	1	1/30	1998	27	26	25
1933	26	24	24	1966	21	20	19	1999	17	16	15
1934	15	13	13	1967	10	9	8	2000	6	4	4
1935	5	3	2	1968	29	28	27	2001	24	23	22
1936	23	21	20	1969	18	16	15	2002	13	12	10
1937	13	12	10	1970	7	6	6	2003	2	1	1/30
1938	2/31	30	29	1971	26	25	24	2004	21	19	18
1939	20	19	19	1972	15	13	13	2005	10	8	8
1940	9	7	7	1973	5	3	2	2006	29	27	27
1941	27	26	26	1974	24	22	21	2007	18	17	15
1942	16	15	15	1975	12	11	11	2008	7	6	5
1943	6	4	4	1976	30	29	29	2009	26	25	24
1944	24	22	22	1977	19	18	18	2010	15	14	14
1945	14	12	11	1978	9	7	7	2011	5	3	3
1946	3	2	1/30	1979	27	26	26	2012	22	21	20
1947	21	20	19	1980	16	15	14	2013	12	10	10
1948	11	9	9	1981	6	4	4	2014	1/31	30	29
1949	29	28	27	1982	24	23	21	2015	20	19	18

TABLE 2   MOON TABLE 3

DAY	APR	MAY	M/D	J	K	L	M	N	O	P
1	J	M	0	AR	TA	TA	TA	GE	GE	GE
2	J	M	1	TA	TA	TA	GE	GE	GE	CA
3	J	M	2	TA	TA	GE	GE	GE	CA	CA
4	J	M	3	TA	GE	GE	GE	CA	CA	CA
5	J	M	4	GE	GE	GE	CA	CA	CA	LE
6	J	M	5	GE	CA	CA	CA	LE	LE	LE
7	J	M	6	CA	CA	CA	LE	LE	LE	VI
8	J	M	7	CA	CA	LE	LE	LE	VI	VI
9	J	M	8	CA	LE	LE	LE	VI	VI	VI
10	J	M	9	LE	LE	VI	VI	VI	LI	LI
11	K	M	10	LE	VI	VI	VI	LI	LI	LI
12	K	N	11	VI	VI	VI	LI	LI	SC	SC
13	K	N	12	VI	VI	LI	LI	LI	SC	SC
14	K	N	13	VI	LI	LI	LI	SC	SC	SC
15	K	N	14	LI	LI	LI	SC	SC	SA	SA
16	K	N	15	LI	SC	SC	SC	SA	SA	SA
17	K	N	16	SC	SC	SC	SA	SA	SA	CP
18	K	N	17	SC	SC	SA	SA	SA	CP	CP
19	K	N	18	SC	SA	SA	SA	CP	CP	CP
20	K	N	19	SA	SA	SA	CP	CP	CP	AQ
21	L	N	20	SA	CP	CP	CP	AQ	AQ	AQ
22	L	O	21	CP	CP	CP	AQ	AQ	AQ	PI
23	L	O	22	CP	CP	AQ	AQ	AQ	PI	PI
24	L	O	23	CP	AQ	AQ	AQ	PI	PI	PI
25	L	O	24	AQ	AQ	AQ	PI	PI	PI	AR
26	L	O	25	AQ	PI	PI	PI	AR	AR	AR
27	L	O	26	PI	PI	PI	AR	AR	AR	TA
28	L	O	27	PI	PI	AR	AR	AR	TA	TA
29	L	O	28	PI	AR	AR	AR	TA	TA	TA
30	L	O	29	AR	AR	AR	TA	TA	TA	GE
31	–	O								

AR = Aries, TA = Taurus, GE = Gemini, CA = Cancer, LE = Leo, VI = Virgo,
LI = Libra, SC = Scorpio, SA = Sagittarius, CP = Capricorn, AQ = Aquarius, PI = Pisces

MOON SIGNS

Moon in Aries

You have a strong imagination, courage, determination and a desire to do things in your own way and forge your own path through life.

Originality is a key attribute; you are seldom stuck for ideas although your mind is changeable and you could take the time to focus on individual tasks. Often quick-tempered, you take orders from few people and live life at a fast pace. Avoid health problems by taking regular time out for rest and relaxation.

Emotionally, it is important that you talk to those you are closest to and work out your true feelings. Once you discover that people are there to help, there is less necessity for you to do everything yourself.

Moon in Taurus

The Moon in Taurus gives you a courteous and friendly manner, which means you are likely to have many friends.

The good things in life mean a lot to you, as Taurus is an Earth sign that delights in experiences which please the senses. Hence you are probably a lover of good food and drink, which may in turn mean you need to keep an eye on the bathroom scales, especially as looking good is also important to you.

Emotionally you are fairly stable and you stick by your own standards. Taureans do not respond well to change. Intuition also plays an important part in your life.

Moon in Gemini

You have a warm-hearted character, sympathetic and eager to help others. At times reserved, you can also be articulate and chatty: this is part of the paradox of Gemini, which always brings duplicity to the nature. You are interested in current affairs, have a good intellect, and are good company and likely to have many friends. Most of your friends have a high opinion of you and would be ready to defend you should the need arise. However, this is usually unnecessary, as you are quite capable of defending yourself in any verbal confrontation.

Travel is important to your inquisitive mind and you find intellectual stimulus in mixing with people from different cultures. You also gain much from reading, writing and the arts but you do need plenty of rest and relaxation in order to avoid fatigue.

Moon in Cancer

The Moon in Cancer at the time of birth is a fortunate position as Cancer is the Moon's natural home. This means that the qualities of compassion and understanding given by the Moon are especially enhanced in your nature, and you are friendly and sociable and cope well with emotional pressures. You cherish home and family life, and happily do the domestic tasks. Your surroundings are important to you and you hate squalor and filth. You are likely to have a love of music and poetry.

Your basic character, although at times changeable like the Moon itself, depends on symmetry. You aim to make your surroundings comfortable and harmonious, for yourself and those close to you.

Moon in Leo

The best qualities of the Moon and Leo come together to make you warm-hearted, fair, ambitious and self-confident. With good organisational abilities, you invariably rise to a position of responsibility in your chosen career. This is fortunate as you don't enjoy being an 'also-ran' and would rather be an important part of a small organisation than a menial in a large one.

You should be lucky in love, and happy, provided you put in the effort to make a comfortable home for yourself and those close to you. It is likely that you will have a love of pleasure, sport, music and literature. Life brings you many rewards, most of them as a direct result of your own efforts, although you may be luckier than average and ready to make the best of any situation.

Moon in Virgo

You are endowed with good mental abilities and a keen receptive memory, but you are never ostentatious or pretentious. Naturally quite reserved, you still have many friends, especially of the opposite sex. Marital relationships must be discussed carefully and worked at so that they remain harmonious, as personal attachments can be a problem if you do not give them your full attention.

Talented and persevering, you possess artistic qualities and are a good homemaker. Earning your honours through genuine merit, you work long and hard towards your objectives but show little pride in your achievements. Many short journeys will be undertaken in your life.

Moon in Libra

With the Moon in Libra you are naturally popular and make friends easily. People like you, probably more than you realise, you bring fun to a party and are a natural diplomat. For all its good points, Libra is not the most stable of astrological signs and, as a result, your emotions can be a little unstable too. Therefore, although the Moon in Libra is said to be good for love and marriage, your Sun sign and Rising sign will have an important effect on your emotional and loving qualities.

You must remember to relate to others in your decision-making. Co-operation is crucial because Libra represents the 'balance' of life that can only be achieved through harmonious relationships. Conformity is not easy for you because Libra, an Air sign, likes its independence.

Moon in Scorpio

Some people might call you pushy. In fact, all you really want to do is to live life to the full and protect yourself and your family from the pressures of life. Take care to avoid giving the impression of being sarcastic or impulsive and use your energies wisely and constructively.

You have great courage and you invariably achieve your goals by force of personality and sheer effort. You are fond of mystery and are good at predicting the outcome of situations and events. Travel experiences can be beneficial to you.

You may experience problems if you do not take time to examine your motives in a relationship, and also if you allow jealousy, always a feature of Scorpio, to cloud your judgement.

Moon in Sagittarius

The Moon in Sagittarius helps to make you a generous individual with humanitarian qualities and a kind heart. Restlessness may be intrinsic as your mind is seldom still. Perhaps because of this, you have a need for change that could lead you to several major moves during your adult life. You are not afraid to stand your ground when you know your judgement is right, you speak directly and have good intuition.

At work you are quick, efficient and versatile and so you make an ideal employee. You need work to be intellectually demanding and do not enjoy tedious routines.

In relationships, you anger quickly if faced with stupidity or deception, though you are just as quick to forgive and forget. Emotionally, there are times when your heart rules your head.

37

Moon in Capricorn

The Moon in Capricorn makes you popular and likely to come into the public eye in some way. The watery Moon is not entirely comfortable in the Earth sign of Capricorn and this may lead to some difficulties in the early years of life. An initial lack of creative ability and indecision must be overcome before the true qualities of patience and perseverance inherent in Capricorn can show through.

You have good administrative ability and are a capable worker, and if you are careful you can accumulate wealth. But you must be cautious and take professional advice in partnerships, as you are open to deception. You may be interested in social or welfare work, which suit your organisational skills and sympathy for others.

Moon in Aquarius

The Moon in Aquarius makes you an active and agreeable person with a friendly, easy-going nature. Sympathetic to the needs of others, you flourish in a laid-back atmosphere. You are broad-minded, fair and open to suggestion, although sometimes you have an unconventional quality which others can find hard to understand.

You are interested in the strange and curious, and in old articles and places. You enjoy trips to these places and gain much from them. Political, scientific and educational work interests you and you might choose a career in science or technology.

Money-wise, you make gains through innovation and concentration and Lunar Aquarians often tackle more than one job at a time. In love you are kind and honest.

Moon in Pisces

You have a kind, sympathetic nature, somewhat retiring at times, but you always take account of others' feelings and help when you can.

Personal relationships may be problematic, but as life goes on you can learn from your experiences and develop a better understanding of yourself and the world around you.

You have a fondness for travel, appreciate beauty and harmony and hate disorder and strife. You may be fond of literature and would make a good writer or speaker yourself. You have a creative imagination and may come across as an incurable romantic. You have strong intuition, maybe bordering on a mediumistic quality, which sets you apart from the mass. You may not be rich in cash terms, but your personal gifts are worth more than gold.

TAURUS IN LOVE

Discover how compatible in love you are with people from the same and other signs of the zodiac. Five stars equals a match made in heaven!

Taurus meets Taurus

A certainty for complete success or absolute failure. Taurus has enough self-knowledge to recognise the strengths of a fellow Taurean, so these two can live in harmony. Both will be tidy and live in comfortable surroundings. Two Taureans seldom argue and will be good friends. But something may be lacking – a spark that doesn't ignite. Passion is important and Taurus reflects, rather than creates it. The prognosis is good, but someone must turn the heat up to get things really cooking. Star rating: ****

Taurus meets Gemini

Gemini people can infuriate the generally steady Taurean nature as they are so untidy, which is a complete reversal of the Taurean ethos. At first this won't matter; Mr or Miss Gemini is enchanting, entertaining and very different. But time will tell, and that's why this potential relationship only has two stars. There is hope, however, because Taurus can curb some of the excesses of the Twins, whilst Gemini is capable of preventing the Bull from taking itself too seriously. Star rating: **

Taurus meets Cancer

This pair will have the tidiest house in the street – every stick of furniture in place, and no errant blade of grass daring to spoil the lawn. But things inside the relationship might not be quite so ship-shape as both signs need, but don't offer, encouragement. There's plenty of affection, but few incentives for mutual progress. This might not prevent material success, but an enduring relationship isn't based on money alone. Passion is essential, and both parties need to realise and aim for that. Star rating: **

Taurus meets Leo

Here we find a generally successful pairing, which frequently leads to an enduring relationship. Taurus needs stimulation which Leo is happy to offer, while Leo responds well to the Bull's sense of order. The essence of the relationship is balance, but it may be achieved with wild swings of the scales on the way, so don't expect a quiet life, though this pair will enjoy a reconciliation after an argument! Material success is probable and, as both like children, a family is likely. Star rating: ***

Taurus meets Virgo

This is a difficult basis for a successful relationship, and yet it often works. Both signs are from the Earth element, so have a common-sense approach to life. They have a mutual understanding, and share many interests. Taurus understands and copes well with Virgo's fussy nature, while Virgo revels in the Bull's tidy and artistic qualities. Both sides are committed to achieving lasting material success. There won't be fireworks, and the match may lack a certain 'spiritual' feel, but as that works both ways it may not be a problem. Star rating: *****

Taurus meets Libra

A happy life is important to both these signs and, as they are both ruled by Venus, they share a common understanding, even though they display themselves so differently. Taurus is quieter than Libra, but can be decisive, and that's what counts. Libra is interested in absolutely everything, an infectious quality when seen through Taurean eyes. The slightly flighty qualities of Libra may lead to jealousy from the Bull. Not an argumentative relationship and one that often works well. There could be many changes of address for this pair. Star rating: ****

Taurus meets Scorpio

Scorpio is deep – very deep – which may be a problem, because Taurus doesn't wear its heart on its sleeve either. It might be difficult for this pair to get together, because neither are naturally inclined to make the first move. Taurus stands in awe of the power and intensity of the Scorpio mind, while the Scorpion is interested in the Bull's affable and friendly qualities, so an enduring relationship could be forged if the couple ever get round to talking. Both are lovers of home and family, which will help to cement a relationship. Star rating: **

Taurus meets Sagittarius

On first impression, Taurus may not like Sagittarius, who may seem brash, and even common, when viewed through the Bull's refined eyes. But there is hope of success because the two signs have so much to offer each other. The Archer is enthralled by the Taurean's natural poise and beauty, while Taurus always needs more basic confidence, which is no problem to Sagittarius who has plenty to spare. Both signs love to travel. There are certain to be ups and downs, but that doesn't prevent an interesting, inspiring and even exciting combination. Star rating: ***

Taurus meets Capricorn

If not quite a match made in heaven, this comes close. Both signs are earthy in nature and that is a promising start. Capricorn is very practical and can make a Taurean's dreams come true. Both are tidy, like to know what is going to happen in a day-to-day sense, and are steady and committed. Taurus loves refinement, which Capricorn accepts and even helps to create. A good prognosis for material success rounds off a relationship that could easily stay the course. The only thing missing is a genuine sense of humour. Star rating: *****

Taurus meets Aquarius

In any relationship of which Aquarius is a part, surprises abound. It is difficult for Taurus to understand the soul-searching, adventurous, changeable Aquarian, but on the positive side, the Bull is adaptable and can respond well to a dose of excitement. Aquarians are kind and react well to the same quality coming back at them. Both are friendly, capable of deep affection and basically quite creative. Unfortunately, though, Taurus simply doesn't know what makes Aquarius tick, which could lead to hidden feelings of isolation. Star rating: **

Taurus meets Pisces

No problem here, unless both parties come from the quieter side of their respective signs. Most of the time Taurus and Pisces would live comfortably together, offering mutual support and deep regard. Taurus can offer the personal qualities that Pisces craves, whilst Pisces understands and copes with the Bull's slightly stubborn qualities. Taurus is likely to travel in Piscean company, so there is a potential for wide-ranging experiences and variety which is essential. There will be some misunderstandings, mainly because Pisces is so deep, but that won't prevent their enduring happiness. Star rating: ***

Taurus meets Aries

This match has been known to work very well. Aries brings dynamism and ambition, while Taurus has the patience to see things through logically. Such complementary views work equally well in a relationship or in an office environment. There is mutual respect, but sometimes a lack of total understanding. The romantic needs of each sign are quite different, but both are still fulfilled. Taurus and Aries can live easily in domestic harmony which is very important but, interestingly, Aries may be the loser in battles of will. Star rating: ***

VENUS:
THE PLANET OF LOVE

If you look up at the sky around sunset or sunrise you will often see Venus in close attendance to the Sun. It is arguably one of the most beautiful sights of all and there is little wonder that historically it became associated with the goddess of love. But although Venus does play an important part in the way you view love and in the way others see you romantically, this is only one of the spheres of influence that it enjoys in your overall character.

Venus has a part to play in the more cultured side of your life and has much to do with your appreciation of art, literature, music and general creativity. Even the way you look is responsive to the part of the zodiac that Venus occupied at the start of your life, though this fact is also down to your Sun sign and Ascending sign. If, at the time you were born, Venus occupied one of the more gregarious zodiac signs, you will be more likely to wear your heart on your sleeve, as well as to be more attracted to entertainment, social gatherings and good company. If on the other hand Venus occupied a quiet zodiac sign at the time of your birth, you would tend to be more retiring and less willing to shine in public situations.

It's good to know what part the planet Venus plays in your life, for it can have a great bearing on the way you appear to the rest of the world and since we all have to mix with others, you can learn to make the very best of what Venus has to offer you.

One of the great complications in the past has always been trying to establish exactly what zodiac position Venus enjoyed when you were born, because the planet is notoriously difficult to track. However, we have solved that problem by creating a table that is exclusive to your Sun sign, which you will find on the following page.

Establishing your Venus sign could not be easier. Just look up the year of your birth on the following page and you will see a sign of the zodiac. This was the sign that Venus occupied in the period covered by your sign in that year. If Venus occupied more than one sign during the period, this is indicated by the date on which the sign changed, and the name of the new sign. For instance, if you were born in 1950, Venus was in Pisces until the 5th May, after which time it was in Aries. If you were born before 5th May your Venus sign is Pisces, if you were born on or after 5th May, your Venus sign is Aries. Once you have established the position of Venus at the time of your birth, you can then look in the pages which follow to see how this has a bearing on your life as a whole.

43

1917 TAURUS / 16.5 GEMINI
1918 PISCES / 7.5 ARIES
1919 GEMINI / 13.5 CANCER
1920 ARIES / 7.5 TAURUS
1921 TAURUS / 27.4 ARIES
1922 TAURUS / 2.5 GEMINI
1923 PISCES / 27.4 ARIES
1924 GEMINI / 7.5 CANCER
1925 TAURUS / 16.5 GEMINI
1926 PISCES / 6.5 ARIES
1927 GEMINI / 12.5 CANCER
1928 ARIES / 6.5 TAURUS
1929 TAURUS / 24.4 ARIES
1930 TAURUS / 1.5 GEMINI
1931 PISCES / 26.4 ARIES
1932 GEMINI / 8.5 CANCER
1933 TAURUS / 15.5 GEMINI
1934 PISCES / 6.5 ARIES
1935 GEMINI / 12.5 CANCER
1936 ARIES / 6.5 TAURUS
1937 TAURUS / 21.4 ARIES
1938 TAURUS / 1.5 GEMINI
1939 PISCES / 26.4 ARIES
1940 GEMINI / 9.5 CANCER
1941 TAURUS / 14.5 GEMINI
1942 PISCES / 6.5 ARIES
1943 GEMINI / 11.5 CANCER
1944 ARIES / 6.5 TAURUS
1945 ARIES
1946 TAURUS / 30.4 GEMINI
1947 PISCES / 25.4 ARIES
1948 GEMINI / 9.5 CANCER
1949 TAURUS / 14.5 GEMINI
1950 PISCES / 5.5 ARIES
1951 GEMINI / 11.5 CANCER
1952 ARIES / 5.5 TAURUS
1953 ARIES
1954 TAURUS / 29.4 GEMINI
1955 PISCES / 25.4 ARIES
1956 GEMINI / 10.5 CANCER
1957 TAURUS / 13.5 GEMINI
1958 PISCES / 5.5 ARIES
1959 GEMINI / 10.5 CANCER
1960 ARIES / 4.5 TAURUS
1961 ARIES
1962 TAURUS / 28.4 GEMINI
1963 PISCES / 24.4 ARIES
1964 GEMINI / 11.5 CANCER
1965 TAURUS / 13.5 GEMINI
1966 PISCES / 5.5 ARIES

1967 GEMINI / 10.5 CANCER
1968 ARIES / 4.5 TAURUS
1969 ARIES
1970 TAURUS / 27.4 GEMINI
1971 PISCES / 24.4 ARIES
1972 GEMINI / 12.5 CANCER
1973 TAURUS / 12.5 GEMINI
1974 PISCES / 4.5 ARIES
1975 GEMINI / 9.5 CANCER
1976 ARIES / 3.5 TAURUS
1977 ARIES
1978 TAURUS / 27.4 GEMINI
1979 PISCES / 23.4 ARIES
1980 GEMINI / 13.5 CANCER
1981 TAURUS / 12.5 GEMINI
1982 PISCES / 4.5 ARIES
1983 GEMINI / 9.5 CANCER
1984 ARIES / 3.5 TAURUS
1985 ARIES
1986 TAURUS / 26.4 GEMINI
1987 PISCES / 23.4 ARIES
1988 GEMINI / 15.5 CANCER
1989 TAURUS / 11.5 GEMINI
1990 PISCES / 4.5 ARIES
1991 GEMINI / 8.5 CANCER
1992 ARIES / 2.5 TAURUS
1993 ARIES
1994 TAURUS / 26.4 GEMINI
1995 PISCES / 22.4 ARIES
1996 GEMINI / 15.5 CANCER
1997 TAURUS / 11.5 GEMINI
1998 PISCES / 3.5 ARIES
1999 GEMINI / 8.5 CANCER
2000 ARIES / 2.5 TAURUS
2001 ARIES
2002 TAURUS / 26.4 GEMINI
2003 PISCES / 22.4 ARIES
2004 GEMINI / 15.5 CANCER
2005 TAURUS / 11.5 GEMINI
2006 PISCES / 3.5 ARIES
2007 GEMINI / 8.5 CANCER
2008 ARIES / 2.5 TAURUS
2009 ARIES
2010 TAURUS / 26.4 GEMINI
2011 PISCES / 22.4 ARIES
2012 PISCES / 22.4 ARIES
2013 PISCES / 3.5 ARIES
2014 PISCES / 3.5 ARIES
2015 GEMINI / 8.5 CANCER

VENUS THROUGH THE ZODIAC SIGNS

Venus in Aries

Amongst other things, the position of Venus in Aries indicates a fondness for travel, music and all creative pursuits. Your nature tends to be affectionate and you would try not to create confusion or difficulty for others if it could be avoided. Many people with this planetary position have a great love of the theatre, and mental stimulation is of the greatest importance. Early romantic attachments are common with Venus in Aries, so it is very important to establish a genuine sense of romantic continuity. Early marriage is not recommended, especially if it is based on sympathy. You may give your heart a little too readily on occasions.

Venus in Taurus

You are capable of very deep feelings and your emotions tend to last for a very long time. This makes you a trusting partner and lover, whose constancy is second to none. In life you are precise and careful and always try to do things the right way. Although this means an ordered life, which you are comfortable with, it can also lead you to be rather too fussy for your own good. Despite your pleasant nature, you are very fixed in your opinions and quite able to speak your mind. Others are attracted to you and historical astrologers always quoted this position of Venus as being very fortunate in terms of marriage. However, if you find yourself involved in a failed relationship, it could take you a long time to trust again.

Venus in Gemini

As with all associations related to Gemini, you tend to be quite versatile, anxious for change and intelligent in your dealings with the world at large. You may gain money from more than one source but you are equally good at spending it. There is an inference here that you are a good communicator, via either the written or the spoken word, and you love to be in the company of interesting people. Always on the look-out for culture, you may also be very fond of music, and love to indulge the curious and cultured side of your nature. In romance you tend to have more than one relationship and could find yourself associated with someone who has previously been a friend or even a distant relative.

45

Venus in Cancer

You often stay close to home because you are very fond of family and enjoy many of your most treasured moments when you are with those you love. Being naturally sympathetic, you will always do anything you can to support those around you, even people you hardly know at all. This charitable side of your nature is your most noticeable trait and is one of the reasons why others are naturally so fond of you. Being receptive and in some cases even psychic, you can see through to the soul of most of those with whom you come into contact. You may not commence too many romantic attachments but when you do give your heart, it tends to be unconditionally.

Venus in Leo

It must become quickly obvious to almost anyone you meet that you are kind, sympathetic and yet determined enough to stand up for anyone or anything that is truly important to you. Bright and sunny, you warm the world with your natural enthusiasm and would rarely do anything to hurt those around you, or at least not intentionally. In romance you are ardent and sincere, though some may find your style just a little overpowering. Gains come through your contacts with other people and this could be especially true with regard to romance, for love and money often come hand in hand for those who were born with Venus in Leo. People claim to understand you, though you are more complex than you seem.

Venus in Virgo

Your nature could well be fairly quiet no matter what your Sun sign might be, though this fact often manifests itself as an inner peace and would not prevent you from being basically sociable. Some delays and even the odd disappointment in love cannot be ruled out with this planetary position, though it's a fact that you will usually find the happiness you look for in the end. Catapulting yourself into romantic entanglements that you know to be rather ill-advised is not sensible, and it would be better to wait before you committed yourself exclusively to any one person. It is the essence of your nature to serve the world at large and through doing so it is possible that you will attract money at some stage in your life.

Venus in Libra

Venus is very comfortable in Libra and bestows upon those people who have this planetary position a particular sort of kindness that is easy to recognise. This is a very good position for all sorts of friendships and also for romantic attachments that usually bring much joy into your life. Few individuals with Venus in Libra would avoid marriage and since you are capable of great depths of love, it is likely that you will find a contented personal life. You like to mix with people of integrity and intelligence but don't take kindly to scruffy surroundings or work that means getting your hands too dirty. Careful speculation, good business dealings and money through marriage all seem fairly likely.

Venus in Scorpio

You are quite open and tend to spend money quite freely, even on those occasions when you don't have very much. Although your intentions are always good, there are times when you get yourself in to the odd scrape and this can be particularly true when it comes to romance, which you may come to late or from a rather unexpected direction. Certainly you have the power to be happy and to make others contented on the way, but you find the odd stumbling block on your journey through life and it could seem that you have to work harder than those around you. As a result of this, you gain a much deeper understanding of the true value of personal happiness than many people ever do, and are likely to achieve true contentment in the end.

Venus in Sagittarius

You are lighthearted, cheerful and always able to see the funny side of any situation. These facts enhance your popularity, which is especially high with members of the opposite sex. You should never have to look too far to find romantic interest in your life, though it is just possible that you might be too willing to commit yourself before you are certain that the person in question is right for you. Part of the problem here extends to other areas of life too. The fact is that you like variety in everything and so can tire of situations that fail to offer it. All the same, if you choose wisely and learn to understand your restless side, then great happiness can be yours.

Venus in Capricorn

The most notable trait that comes from Venus in this position is that it makes you trustworthy and able to take on all sorts of responsibilities in life. People are instinctively fond of you and love you all the more because you are always ready to help those who are in any form of need. Social and business popularity can be yours and there is a magnetic quality to your nature that is particularly attractive in a romantic sense. Anyone who wants a partner for a lover, a spouse and a good friend too would almost certainly look in your direction. Constancy is the hallmark of your nature and unfaithfulness would go right against the grain. You might sometimes be a little too trusting.

Venus in Aquarius

This location of Venus offers a fondness for travel and a desire to try out something new at every possible opportunity. You are extremely easy to get along with and tend to have many friends from varied backgrounds, classes and inclinations. You like to live a distinct sort of life and gain a great deal from moving about, both in a career sense and with regard to your home. It is not out of the question that you could form a romantic attachment to someone who comes from far away or be attracted to a person of a distinctly artistic and original nature. What you cannot stand is jealousy, for you have friends of both sexes and would want to keep things that way.

Venus in Pisces

The first thing people tend to notice about you is your wonderful, warm smile. Being very charitable by nature you will do anything to help others, even if you don't know them well. Much of your life may be spent sorting out situations for other people, but it is very important to feel that you are living for yourself too. In the main, you remain cheerful, and tend to be quite attractive to members of the opposite sex. Where romantic attachments are concerned, you could be drawn to people who are significantly older or younger than yourself or to someone with a unique career or point of view. It might be best for you to avoid marrying whilst you are still very young.

TAURUS:
2014 DIARY PAGES

October 2014

1 WEDNESDAY   *Moon Age Day 7   Moon Sign Sagittarius*

It's important to recognise when you should open your mouth today and when it would be better to keep your counsel. Trends suggest that this would be a very opportune time to welcome people you haven't seen for ages into your life again. Although this could be a distinctly odd day, you need to make the most of the opportunities it offers.

2 THURSDAY   *Moon Age Day 8   Moon Sign Capricorn*

The lure of luxury is very strong at this time, making it an ideal interlude to treat yourself in some way. Any chance to travel should be grabbed with both hands, and you can make great gains through the involvement of friends in your life. All in all, you have everything you need to make the most of a very positive period.

3 FRIDAY   *Moon Age Day 9   Moon Sign Capricorn*

Right now, outdoor activities seem to have a particular reward, though how you use this trend is up to you. Maybe you will show the sporting side of your nature, or choose to take a walk in the fresh air. Meanwhile, it's worth keeping up your efforts to move ahead professionally and seeking advice from some very good friends at this time.

4 SATURDAY   *Moon Age Day 10   Moon Sign Aquarius*

This is an interlude during which attempts to get on well in a practical sense are well accented. Taking all you have learned in the past, it's time to apply your experience to matters in the practical world and come up with answers that show others how clever you are. Avoid being too quick to judge the actions of your friends.

5 SUNDAY ☿ *Moon Age Day 11* *Moon Sign Aquarius*

You have a great deal to gain through your social life and friendships, because both can offer you diversion and interest today. Be willing to confront any issues you have avoided in the past, since you may find they are easier to resolve than you expected. It pays to get jobs you don't like out of the way early.

6 MONDAY ☿ *Moon Age Day 12* *Moon Sign Pisces*

Does it now seem as though your patience is being tried by various matters? This would be an ideal time to throw out anything you no longer need, though this is just as likely to be a state of mind as a piece of old furniture. From a social point of view, the advancing day offers you scope for more contentment than of late.

7 TUESDAY ☿ *Moon Age Day 13* *Moon Sign Pisces*

Beware of coming on too strong, particularly when it comes to a specific personal attachment. Trends encourage you to modify your nature a little in order to accommodate that of someone else, though that doesn't mean you shouldn't show the real you when it matters the most. Dealing with confidences from friends counts for a great deal now.

8 WEDNESDAY ☿ *Moon Age Day 14* *Moon Sign Aries*

Plenty of information is there for the taking at the moment and it is up to you to use it wisely. It's important to listen to all advice, even if in the end you choose to discard some of it. Be willing to show that famous Venusian charm, which can help you to win friends. Influencing the world at large is important now.

9 THURSDAY ☿ *Moon Age Day 15* *Moon Sign Aries*

The more you can do to help others move forward in their own lives, the better you should find that you feel about what is happening to you. The twelfth-house Moon suggests that this may not be the most exciting day you will register this month. Make sure you're ready to capitalise on what's available tomorrow.

10 FRIDAY   ☿   *Moon Age Day 16   Moon Sign Taurus*

If this doesn't turn out to be a Friday to remember, you should ask yourself whether you are trying as hard as you could. All in all, the lunar high offers a mixture of possibilities during its October visit. On a personal level, it assists you to attract much more attention, and to deal with practical matters in a flash.

11 SATURDAY   ☿   *Moon Age Day 17   Moon Sign Taurus*

Material success is the order of the day as the continuing lunar high offers greater incentives and new possibilities. Even if you aren't exactly over the moon about the advancing year and the colder weather, you needn't allow that fact to bother you too much at the moment. The great outdoors is beckoning, so be ready to respond.

12 SUNDAY   ☿   *Moon Age Day 18   Moon Sign Gemini*

Seeking out a variety of interests would suit this weekend's astrological scene, and would certainly be better than sitting around and waiting for life to come to you. Although some jobs might take you longer than you had anticipated, the Taurean need to do things properly is in evidence. A time to seek warmth and support from friends.

13 MONDAY   ☿   *Moon Age Day 19   Moon Sign Gemini*

Trends indicate that you need to take greater care of a specific matter than has been the case in recent days. Perhaps you have a worry about something at home, or an outstanding practical task that needs to be done. Address such matters today but remember that there are many fun-filled opportunities as well. Share yourself out wisely.

14 TUESDAY   ☿   *Moon Age Day 20   Moon Sign Cancer*

Some typically Taurean qualities are emphasised today, especially your possessive tendency. If you know they are around you have an opportunity to do something about them. Friendships have a great deal to offer you now, and could convince you to go that extra mile in order to help someone out of a dilemma.

15 WEDNESDAY ☿ *Moon Age Day 21   Moon Sign Cancer*

It seems that the further you travel today, the better you will enjoy the journey. This is as true in your head as it is in the real world. Treating yourself in some way can also work wonders, and it is clear that you have plenty of charm and diplomacy. All in all you have what it takes to turn this into quite an enjoyable day.

16 THURSDAY ☿ *Moon Age Day 22   Moon Sign Cancer*

If you've been seeking new opportunities for a while, it pays to keep a special eye out today. Routines might be less important at this stage of the month, and there are good reasons to focus instead on the unorthodox in life. Not everything that works for you at present can be easily explained.

17 FRIDAY ☿ *Moon Age Day 23   Moon Sign Leo*

Rather than restricting discussions with others to the everyday subjects of life, why not allow your mind to wander into the realms of the possible? You don't always allow yourself to daydream quite as much as you should, probably because the practical quality of your nature gets in the way. Now you have a chance to talk, and maybe even write, as a visionary.

18 SATURDAY ☿ *Moon Age Day 24   Moon Sign Leo*

Personal relationships count for a great deal under present planetary influences, and some Taurus people might even be at the start of exciting new romances. Even ordinary friends can be the source of great warmth right now, and you should also be on the look-out for some surprising news from the direction of a really close pal.

19 SUNDAY ☿ *Moon Age Day 25   Moon Sign Virgo*

You can't expect to be able to do absolutely everything you would wish today, though you can still look for ways to please yourself. Most important of all, it's worth finding moments – or hours – to get away from the mundane in life and into some sort of excitement, no matter what that might mean to you.

20 MONDAY ☿ *Moon Age Day 26 Moon Sign Virgo*

The spotlight is now on your current need to impose your ideas on others. There is a bit of a difference between this and the attitude that has prevailed for Taurus recently. No matter how hard you try, there are still likely to be certain individuals who simply don't agree with your opinions. Attempting to bulldoze them probably won't help!

21 TUESDAY ☿ *Moon Age Day 27 Moon Sign Virgo*

There are different trends around now. Even if you are still keen to mix and mingle as much as possible on one level, you are also encouraged to display the deeply personal side of Taurus. A suitable compromise might be to spend as much time as you can today talking to and moving about with those you know well and trust intimately.

22 WEDNESDAY ☿ *Moon Age Day 28 Moon Sign Libra*

Opportunities for material progress may well be lacking today, and if this is the case you might well decide to enjoy yourself in a social sense instead. There are good reasons to focus your efforts on your partner, family members or really good friends. The world at large probably doesn't hold that much fascination for you now.

23 THURSDAY ☿ *Moon Age Day 0 Moon Sign Libra*

The key to success today is to open up avenues of communication, after a few days when a somewhat quieter and more restricted approach was called for in terms of your social contacts. Be prepared to make the most of some romantic overtures that are available now. The indications are that these will be from expected directions.

24 FRIDAY ☿ *Moon Age Day 1 Moon Sign Scorpio*

As a new day gets started, you may feel that you are lagging behind the game. This suggests the influence of the lunar low, though it does at least offer you the opportunity to think things through in a more clear and concise way. Creative potential is well accented, especially regarding changes you want to make to your home environment.

25 SATURDAY ☿ *Moon Age Day 2 Moon Sign Scorpio*

The lunar low brings a period during which you might normally decide to take a rest, though other astrological trends now offer you a range of other options. However, beware of starting too many new ventures at this time and keep your efforts to a minimum when it comes to undertaking important financial transactions.

26 SUNDAY *Moon Age Day 3 Moon Sign Scorpio*

The present position of the Moon encourages a rather less decisive approach than would normally be the case. This often happens as the lunar low starts to retreat, and is a temporary phase. Your best response is to check details carefully and to make certain you are not barking up the wrong tree when it comes to a very specific assumption.

27 MONDAY *Moon Age Day 4 Moon Sign Sagittarius*

You can afford to keep yourself on the go for most of today, with travel once again positively highlighted, together with an ability to make gains in new places. Organising yourself might prove a little awkward, though you have scope to bring some humour into the situation. A slightly absentminded element is indicated under present trends.

28 TUESDAY *Moon Age Day 5 Moon Sign Sagittarius*

It pays to channel much of your effort into your work, particularly if you have plenty of energy to tap into. By all means call on some assistance if you find yourself out of your depth at any stage, though it may be that you would prefer to go it alone. That's fine, though beware of being too proud for your own good.

29 WEDNESDAY *Moon Age Day 6 Moon Sign Capricorn*

You can gain a great deal through being out of doors, so get some fresh air today before the winds of winter begin to blow. Taurus people who have organised a late holiday will probably have made a good decision, since being on the move is now well starred. Trends indicate a particular affinity for growing things at present.

30 THURSDAY   *Moon Age Day 7*   *Moon Sign Capricorn*

This is a day on which there are good reasons to keep your eyes wide open. With everything to play for and plenty of enthusiasm when it counts the most, you have a chance to capitalise on one of the most potentially successful working periods of the year. Be sure to tell people the way your mind is working and leave nothing to chance.

31 FRIDAY   *Moon Age Day 8*   *Moon Sign Aquarius*

Make full use of your sharp mind, and realise that most of your intuitive insights are well worth following. One of the most important factors today is the recognition you can gain from others for your good ideas. Take note of the way the world is watching you and be sure to make the most of these very useful trends.

♏ ⊕

November

1 SATURDAY
Moon Age Day 9   Moon Sign Aquarius

House and home are suddenly the focus of attention, assisting you to create the right circumstances for a happy but deliberately restricted sort of weekend. Getting to grips with family issues should be easy, and you also need to find sufficient time for romance to work one or two little wonders in your life.

2 SUNDAY
Moon Age Day 10   Moon Sign Pisces

You can now afford to relax a little and improve your home conditions while you are about it. Commitment to practical issues at work might have to wait, because for today at least the trends encourage you to take a different approach. Don't worry though, because you have scope to change direction in an instant tomorrow.

3 MONDAY
Moon Age Day 11   Moon Sign Pisces

Now is the time to seek out some hopeful news regarding personal objectives and wishes. You can't expect everyone to be on your side today, especially at work, though you should still be able to forge a positive path and impress a few important people on the way. Why not leave some time free later for romantic moments?

4 TUESDAY
Moon Age Day 12   Moon Sign Aries

Travel could well be a natural aspect of life at the moment. Maybe you have decided that the time is right to visit a relative or a friend who lives at a distance. There is a certain restlessness in the air that dissuades you from staying in the same place. Utilising and capitalising on this wanderlust counts for a great deal now.

5 WEDNESDAY   *Moon Age Day 13   Moon Sign Aries*

Along comes a time that could prove to be particularly favourable for social adventures and for general co-operation. If you're willing to compromise, you stand a chance of convincing others to relinquish a great deal of the control of situations to you. Taurus may not see itself as a natural leader, but those around you respect both your views and actions.

6 THURSDAY   *Moon Age Day 14   Moon Sign Taurus*

As the lunar high arrives, your high spirits and sense of humour should be clearly on display. It's up to you to ensure that everything is a laugh today, and this assists you to deal with even tricky situations in a flash. Does it appear that other people are naturally compromising in their attitudes? Perhaps this is down to the way you are acting yourself.

7 FRIDAY   *Moon Age Day 15   Moon Sign Taurus*

There could be one or two shortcuts to success for Taurus now, especially if you keep your eyes open. At the end of this working week it's a question of trying to get authority figures on your side and being willing to seek help from friends. It pays to concentrate on a specific matter early in the day and generalities later.

8 SATURDAY   *Moon Age Day 16   Moon Sign Taurus*

This is a good time to push your luck and certainly not a period during which you will make headway by hiding your talents or your intentions. Allow your light to shine brightly and have confidence in your ability to get things done. Financial incentives are especially well accented, as are the romantic prospects of this positive day.

9 SUNDAY   *Moon Age Day 17   Moon Sign Gemini*

Handling several different tasks at the same time shouldn't be difficult right now, though it's important to be just a little careful that you don't tire yourself too much. This is Sunday after all, and is supposed to be a time when you get some rest. Resolving any confusion over personal matters is part of what today is about.

10 MONDAY *Moon Age Day 18 Moon Sign Gemini*

Trends assist you to show what good company you can be today, and this in turn should help you to increase your popularity no end. There's nothing wrong with keeping up with invitations that come along, though if there are too many, you'll need to be selective. A busy phase is on offer, with new incentives available all the time.

11 TUESDAY *Moon Age Day 19 Moon Sign Cancer*

It's easy to allow your desire to make important changes to your life to be affected by the attitude and actions of family members or friends at the moment. Patience is your best response, a fact that also seems to be true at work. Fortunately you come from a zodiac sign that has patience written all the way through it.

12 WEDNESDAY *Moon Age Day 20 Moon Sign Cancer*

This has potential to be one of the best days of the month for simply pursuing your own interests and desires. Convincing your partner and family members to allow you as much leeway as you wish can make all the difference to your endeavour. You might even be able to persuade them to join in with whatever you suggest.

13 THURSDAY *Moon Age Day 21 Moon Sign Leo*

Though getting on with others is still possible, it can be tricky if they are rather less decisive than you would wish. Beware of trying to please too many people because it is unlikely to work. There is much to be said for allowing those you love to make their own mistakes, since it is probably the only way they will learn valuable lessons.

14 FRIDAY *Moon Age Day 22 Moon Sign Leo*

Although you can still afford to focus a good deal on your own needs, you are also encouraged to show a greater sense of responsibility towards others as today wears on. There is nothing at all wrong with feathering your own nest, as long as you remember that you are not alone. Avoid getting into pointless discussions, especially at work.

15 SATURDAY   *Moon Age Day 23   Moon Sign Leo*

Getting yourself properly organised can be very important, right from the start of today. There are gains to be made from showing you've done your homework, particularly at work. There are strong romantic trends around right now and this would be a good day to let someone know exactly how you feel about them, even though this takes courage.

16 SUNDAY   *Moon Age Day 24   Moon Sign Virgo*

Trends herald a great thirst for adventure today and a determination that is stronger than Taurus has registered for a month or two. It's worth getting as much done as you can because your level of energy is emphasised and your sense of purpose second to none. Be prepared to defer family arrangements in order to accommodate your state of mind.

17 MONDAY   *Moon Age Day 25   Moon Sign Virgo*

There is a strong possibility of personal disagreements around today, and these need to be avoided if at all possible. It can certainly be annoying if others are throwing their weight about, and this is a situation that won't assist you progress. Try to remain calm and concentrate on your own tasks rather than worrying about everything else.

18 TUESDAY   *Moon Age Day 26   Moon Sign Libra*

Business and material matters look extremely favourable around now, with plenty of potential for excitement and a good deal of popularity to be gained. This is a time to strike whilst the iron is hot, and to seek the assistance you need right on your own doorstep. Make sure family members are amenable to your ideas.

19 WEDNESDAY   *Moon Age Day 27   Moon Sign Libra*

You have what it takes to put yourself in the social limelight at present, and that's a position that is both exciting and somewhat unnerving. Even if you know what you are talking about and feel quite confident, there is always the chance, in your mind at least, that you might make some sort of gaffe.

20 THURSDAY   *Moon Age Day 28   Moon Sign Libra*

Brand new projects should be taking shape, your attitude ought to be very positive, and you should be getting into the groove as far as your social life is concerned. You have everything you need to ensure that life is plain sailing at the moment, and needn't allow anything to prevent you from breaking through barriers that have surrounded you for while.

21 FRIDAY   *Moon Age Day 29   Moon Sign Scorpio*

The lunar low could shine a spotlight on a rather thorny problem today, and a fairly circumspect approach will be required in order to deal with it. Why not seek some help? The rather insular Taurus approach at the moment is all very well, though you shouldn't feel that asking for assistance is beneath your dignity.

22 SATURDAY   *Moon Age Day 0   Moon Sign Scorpio*

Progress may be steady at best because you have the lunar low to contend with for the rest of today. A slower interlude could actually be very welcome, particularly if you have been constantly on the go for a while now. All Taureans need rest and recuperation at some stage, because that is what gets you thinking and planning.

23 SUNDAY   *Moon Age Day 1   Moon Sign Sagittarius*

The material side of your life may feel, for one reason or another, to be slightly less clear-cut today. Some decisive action is the order of the day, but a slight hesitancy is indicated that wasn't around during the last couple of days. There are good reasons to rely on a family member or a friend for the support you need.

24 MONDAY   *Moon Age Day 2   Moon Sign Sagittarius*

There is potential for you to take advantage of a far easier and more co-operative atmosphere which is developing at home. Coincidentally, home is also the place where you can gain most comfort at the moment. If the big, wide world seems slightly intimidating, use the start of the new week to get your bearings again, and try to remain confident.

25 TUESDAY   *Moon Age Day 3   Moon Sign Capricorn*

The emphasis at present is on your enhanced vision and your ability to be creative. Today is favourable for travelling and for learning anything. There are definite gains to be made from educational processes and from being involved in activities outside your work. Excitement seems to stand around every corner.

26 WEDNESDAY   *Moon Age Day 4   Moon Sign Capricorn*

Assertiveness is now the order of the day, and this may come as a surprise to certain individuals with whom you interact. There are several good planetary reasons why it's important to you now to get your own way in most matters. With Mars in a very strong position, you shouldn't have any trouble at all in getting your message across.

27 THURSDAY   *Moon Age Day 5   Moon Sign Aquarius*

You have scope to find a good deal more warmth in your love life around this time than has been the case of late. Part of this is down to your willingness to accept a position as number one – in someone's estimation at least. You might be surprised at some of the compliments that you can attract, but you genuinely do deserve them.

28 FRIDAY   *Moon Age Day 6   Moon Sign Aquarius*

Practical matters seem to be your best area of success today, with domestic and personal issues turning just a little icy in one way or another. Keep your eyes open for a great big chunk of goodwill that is available from one direction or another, since this should turn out to be especially useful at the moment.

29 SATURDAY   *Moon Age Day 7   Moon Sign Pisces*

Digging deep in order to get to the root of any particular problem is all very well, though you may in the end decide that it probably isn't worth it in some cases. Remaining cool, calm and collected is the best way of winning through any competition. Mutual co-operation may be more difficult today, especially with friends.

30 SUNDAY
Moon Age Day 8   Moon Sign Pisces

Getting out and about is advisable this weekend. If you stay in the same place too much, boredom is more or less guaranteed, and there is much to be gained from being flexible. If there's an issue that you have kept to yourself for a while, today's trends encourage you to seek help from friends to address it.

December

2014

1 MONDAY
Moon Age Day 9   Moon Sign Pisces

Your strength lies in your willingness to take the initiative more than usual today, and that helps you to get yourself noticed. This is a time when you can get a great deal done, even if your attitude towards some situations is rather unusual. Don't rush your fences because there should be plenty of time to get jobs sorted properly.

2 TUESDAY
Moon Age Day 10   Moon Sign Aries

If social matters are not as rewarding today as you hoped, it pays to ask yourself why. The attitude of others may hold some of the answers, particularly if it is not what you had come to expect. Even if there is plenty to keep you occupied all day, you do need some space to simply sit and think, an essential for Taurus now and again.

3 WEDNESDAY
Moon Age Day 11   Moon Sign Aries

Give and take could now be in short supply, especially from your loved ones. Although the giving side of your nature is to the fore at present, you can't necessarily expect the same attitude in return. Maybe you are concentrating on the wrong people and should be looking towards friends, rather than relatives.

4 THURSDAY
Moon Age Day 12   Moon Sign Taurus

Clear thinking is quite vital today, and with everything to play for you have what it takes to make this one of the most progressive days of the month. You may already be getting your head around plans for Christmas, and a general long-term view, though good in some ways, might prevent immediate benefits from the lunar high.

5 FRIDAY
Moon Age Day 13   Moon Sign Taurus

The major decisions you are faced with today could well provide you with scope for both excitement and success. There will rarely be a better time to take your courage in your own hands and to go for it. With plenty of assistance when you need it the most, this is the sort of time when Taurus can really show its mettle.

6 SATURDAY
Moon Age Day 14   Moon Sign Gemini

The romantic view of life is fine, but trends suggest that it isn't your best approach today. Now is a time to be hard-nosed and very practical. You are not letting others down as long as you bear their future in mind too, so you need to ensure that this is what you are doing. All the same, be ready for some temporary recriminations.

7 SUNDAY
Moon Age Day 15   Moon Sign Gemini

The impressionable and sensitive side of your character is emphasised this Sunday, and there's nothing wrong with showing this to the people you mix with for most of the time. Even if the day is quite busy, you need to find moments during which you can stop and think. Rushing around might spoil much of what today is about.

8 MONDAY
Moon Age Day 16   Moon Sign Cancer

You should be able to get the best from communications today and can gain from simply speaking your mind. Even if not everyone agrees with what you are saying, it's a question of persuading them that you have the right to speak out. What matters the most is that you get yourself well and truly noticed.

9 TUESDAY
Moon Age Day 17   Moon Sign Cancer

It may be difficult to maintain the pace of developments in your life generally today, and there's a risk that you might be rather too outspoken for you own good. However, trends are more favourable on the romantic front and it's time to get others to take notice of you. It is better they see your slightly fractious side than not see you at all.

10 WEDNESDAY   *Moon Age Day 18   Moon Sign Cancer*

A good clear-out would be no bad thing at the moment, particularly because Christmas is just around the corner. Speaking of the festive season, are you fully prepared? It's worth another check because a slightly absentminded element is indicated for Taurus at the moment. Socially speaking, the day improves as it ages.

11 THURSDAY   *Moon Age Day 19   Moon Sign Leo*

Perhaps it is now time for a change of scene? You won't get too far today sitting around with your feet up, but neither should you be overdoing it in a social sense. The practical qualities inherent in your zodiac sign now come into focus, encouraging you to remain fully active and engaged throughout the day.

12 FRIDAY   *Moon Age Day 20   Moon Sign Leo*

You have what it takes to hit most of your goals today, this should help you to make this a generally satisfying end to the working week. Although the odd setback in personal terms can't be ruled out, in a general sense you can afford to remain optimistic. Your personality proves to be especially warm at present.

13 SATURDAY   *Moon Age Day 21   Moon Sign Virgo*

Getting on very well with others counts for a great deal as the day wears on, and you shouldn't have any problem at all compromising with colleagues and friends. There is a kind of warmth around now that you might put down to the approaching Christmas season, but this also relates to present astrological trends.

14 SUNDAY   *Moon Age Day 22   Moon Sign Virgo*

If you feel slightly unsure about any of your current objectives around this time, why not check your details carefully before proceeding? This would be a favourable day to make a journey, especially if it is to see someone you haven't been in touch with for a while. The attitude of your partner might take some working out now. Patience is the key.

15 MONDAY
Moon Age Day 23   Moon Sign Virgo

Financial and practical issues ought to be plain sailing, and a few positive planetary trends give you all the assistance you need to make significant progress when it matters the most. It's natural for rules and regulations to get on your nerves at present, because even if you recognise their value, they probably get in the way of progress.

16 TUESDAY
Moon Age Day 24   Moon Sign Libra

You might have to consider reorganising your social life in some way today, particularly if other people are unavailable for one reason or another. Try to remain flexible. This isn't always easy for the sign of Taurus, but it would work wonders right now. A deeply independent streak starts to show itself at this time.

17 WEDNESDAY
Moon Age Day 25   Moon Sign Libra

Today offers an opportunity to look into specific private matters, and you might even discover that things are not quite what they have seemed. All in all, it's worth keeping your detective head on at present, and expect to feel that you cannot settle until you have arrived at the truth of any matter that captivates your curiosity.

18 THURSDAY
Moon Age Day 26   Moon Sign Scorpio

Certain aspects of life could well be trying your patience, which wouldn't be too surprising now that the lunar low is around. Your best approach is to remain as calm and collected as you can. Showing a good deal of self-discipline if you feel you are under threat can work wonders now, and can balance the over-sensitive side of your nature.

19 FRIDAY
Moon Age Day 27   Moon Sign Scorpio

This has potential to be a favourable day for all romantic developments, especially if a new attachment has come along recently. In a less personal sense you need to remember that not everyone may be quite what they seem. It's worth taking extra care before signing documents or entering into any sort of binding commitment.

20 SATURDAY   *Moon Age Day 28   Moon Sign Sagittarius*

Be ready to take a more prominent position in a social sense now, which may not be too difficult as Christmas draws nigh. With plenty to play for and fun and games definitely up your street, getting together with friends has a great deal to offer. You tend to perform to an audience at the moment.

21 SUNDAY   *Moon Age Day 29   Moon Sign Sagittarius*

Once again you have the chance to step into the limelight in some way today, and should certainly be happy to make up for lost time. You can't expect everyone to be on your side at the moment, but if people seem grumpy, that's their problem and not yours. You have a love of life and you needn't let anything stop that.

22 MONDAY   *Moon Age Day 0   Moon Sign Sagittarius*

Frustrations are a distinct possibility at this time, particularly in terms of someone close to home. Co-operation is the key, though it may not be at all easy. Don't be too quick to apportion blame if something goes wrong and stay calm at all costs. The real problem at the moment is getting on with what you most want to do.

23 TUESDAY   *Moon Age Day 1   Moon Sign Capricorn*

Does it appear that loved ones, or at least some of them, are willing to take a more dominant role in decision making? This should be welcomed – unless it threatens your own position. There is a lesson to be learned here. You cannot encourage others to be more independent and then retreat when it doesn't suit you.

24 WEDNESDAY   *Moon Age Day 2   Moon Sign Capricorn*

Anything that contributes to a sense of variety is what you should be seeking on Christmas Eve. You could easily become bored, and need to feel that life is stimulating. Taxing your brain is no problem, and you might even be doing this deliberately. An ideal day to spend time with your partner and to whisper the right words at the most appropriate time.

25 THURSDAY *Moon Age Day 3   Moon Sign Aquarius*

Christmas Day has plenty to offer, even if you feel rushed off your feet in one way or another. Beware of taking anything for granted because it's important to check and recheck all details at this time. It's up to you to make sure fun is on the agenda, and this might involve taking last-minute decisions on the social alternatives available.

26 FRIDAY *Moon Age Day 4   Moon Sign Aquarius*

There are some demands that could prove to be an uphill struggle today, and it has to be said that Boxing Day is unlikely to offer the incentives that were available yesterday. If you fall back on to your nostalgic side, you can still enjoy yourself. Why not watch a good film on the television or take a steady stroll around the park?

27 SATURDAY *Moon Age Day 5   Moon Sign Pisces*

Domestic disputes can't be ruled out, even during the festive period, and you might decide it is better to retreat rather than to cause an argument. All in all, you may choose to spend time with friends rather than family at the moment. By all means focus on work issues, even if there is nothing you can do directly during the holiday period.

28 SUNDAY *Moon Age Day 6   Moon Sign Pisces*

There are good ideas available, some of which come as a result of exchanges of opinion. Even if you don't agree directly with everything that others are saying, it is in these slight disagreements that the future can be forged. Confidence is well accented at the moment, and you clearly know how to approach anyone.

29 MONDAY *Moon Age Day 7   Moon Sign Aries*

You have scope for plenty of fun around now, since trends highlight the strength of your powers of attraction. The accent is on pleasure, and you might even decide to indulge in a number of extravagances that you would normally fight shy of. There probably isn't much point in starting any new practical ventures right at this time.

30 TUESDAY
Moon Age Day 8   Moon Sign Aries

There are new possibilities coming along to assist you to broaden your horizons, and even if the practicalities of life are somewhat on hold for the moment, there's nothing to stop you looking ahead and planning. There are good reasons to focus your attention firmly on the New Year and what it has to offer.

31 WEDNESDAY
Moon Age Day 9   Moon Sign Taurus

A surge of real energy is there for the taking as the lunar high arrives, and this should assist you to pep up the party possibilities at this time. There are possible gains through relationships and plenty of scope for new friendships that you can form at this time. Give yourself to the moment and party for all you are worth this evening.

TAURUS:
2015 DIARY PAGES

TAURUS:
YOUR YEAR IN BRIEF

The coming year may not offer you everything you are looking for, but the fact is that you find it to be both useful and, on occasions, more exciting than 2014 turned out to be. Almost from the word go you are looking for new horizons and situations that you can turn to your advantage, especially during January and February, as you strive to improve your financial lot. You should also find this to be an ideal time for making new friends. However, you'll have to wait until later in the year for dynamism to come along.

By March, you have the feeling that things are generally going quite well, though you could notice a slight sense of dissatisfaction that can only be dealt with by keeping busy. April brings a sense of joy from things well done and also offers better social prospects, together with more responsibility at work, perhaps improving your finances.

As May arrives, you are in the thick of things, anxious to make a favourable impression and also gaining significantly from the fact that financial and personal aspects are going your way. May especially marks a time when you can achieve more and you could find people singling you out for positive treatment.

July offers challenges and the chance to overcome obstacles that may have got in your way earlier. You are friendly to just about everyone you meet, and the more intellectual and creative potential within your nature is showing more. These trends continue during August, but this is a more dislocated month that is likely to bring travel and a slight inability to concentrate on the practicalities of life. Friends should be especially helpful around this time.

With September and October comes a slowing of your life and potential generally. This is no bad thing, because you will have time to stand and think, something that could be missing from a good part of the year. This is vital to the Taurus individual, because you need to plan ahead and to take stock of situations on a regular basis. Once again you should find love shining brightly through your life, and friends will be especially attentive.

As the year draws to its close and you look back at the progress you have made, you should be fairly happy. November is busy, with plenty to keep you occupied and the chance of a new start or advancement at work. December will be given over more to having fun and you should really enjoy the Christmas period this year. Love is the most important factor for many during the last week of the year and you will also be heaping far more attention on family members.

♉

January
2015

1 THURSDAY
Moon Age Day 11 Moon Sign Taurus

The Moon is now in your own zodiac sign of Taurus. With the lunar high, there is potential for a sudden and even unexpected burst of energy on your part, and it would be hard to avoid the conclusion that Lady Luck is also on your side. Put in your best effort now for maximum results.

2 FRIDAY
Moon Age Day 12 Moon Sign Gemini

It might be wise to be cautious in group situations at the moment, if only because there are one or two people you don't get on with all that well. A good old chat with good friends might inspire you, so take advantage of opportunities to get involved in subjects that are really close to your heart.

3 SATURDAY
Moon Age Day 13 Moon Sign Gemini

For most of the time you will show yourself to be warm and cheerful – just right for taking the bull by the horns in a romantic sense. You won't lack popularity and can show the world at large what a happy-go-lucky little Bull you are. Routines might get on your nerves, so leave them to others if you can.

4 SUNDAY
Moon Age Day 14 Moon Sign Gemini

There is a chance today for some fulfilling encounters and it is clear that you are feeling much more optimistic now. You can bring romantic issues to a peak and may also find that you have an admirer you didn't previously suspect. It is also likely that an acquaintance could become much more.

5 MONDAY
Moon Age Day 15 Moon Sign Cancer

The time is right to seek out stimulating experiences with your friends. This will bring out the best in you and others, and you certainly should not go short of attention under present planetary trends. Later in the day, you might have to get to grips with a personal issue, but try a little conversation to settle things nicely.

6 TUESDAY
Moon Age Day 16 Moon Sign Cancer

Your strength lies in your popularity with others today. You are likely to be on a real winner in your social life, as it seems as though you are never short of a good idea for having fun. Revel in the chance to travel, but be wary of being too quick to take command in settings you neither understand nor like.

7 WEDNESDAY
Moon Age Day 17 Moon Sign Leo

The challenge today may be to keep on top of things in a professional sense. Although it is likely that details could go wrong, you remain particularly good at thinking on your feet. This is so much the case that you can turn a disadvantage around completely and impress more than a few people on the way.

8 THURSDAY
Moon Age Day 18 Moon Sign Leo

You continue to be in the know when it comes to getting your own way. The signs are that you are also quite intuitive at the moment, so you could have a particularly good idea of the way others are likely to behave. This gives you a definite edge and an ability to judge what moves to make in order to feather your nest both now and for later.

9 FRIDAY
Moon Age Day 19 Moon Sign Virgo

This would be one of the best times of the month for getting involved in a new kind of partnership. You co-operate particularly well and don't get too hung up on details or specifics right now. It should certainly be very much easier than usual to give someone else the benefit of the doubt. Try to conserve your energy.

10 SATURDAY   *Moon Age Day 20   Moon Sign Virgo*

Things are not going to be quite as atmospheric in romantic relationships as you might wish and your own present practical approach might have something to do with the situation. The poetic Taurus is taking a holiday and you will have to work especially hard at the moment if you want to sweep someone off his or her feet.

11 SUNDAY   *Moon Age Day 21   Moon Sign Virgo*

The harder you look today, the greater is the chance that you will see things that please you. This is no time to hide in a corner. Instead, you need to show your bright and interesting qualities if you want to get on well. The weekend is a great time to show how good you are at doing something specific.

12 MONDAY   *Moon Age Day 22   Moon Sign Libra*

When it comes to your personal life, you could hardly be in a better position than the one with which you are presented on this January Monday. Everything should come together to offer you the best chance possible of making a favourable impression on prospective sweethearts. Don't be slow when it comes to handing out compliments.

13 TUESDAY   *Moon Age Day 23   Moon Sign Libra*

As you get down to brass tacks today, it becomes quite obvious that you are in the market to make more money. This might not mesh with the ideas of others, who think they have more right to the cash than you do. The result has to be some sort of competition, but if you are determined you are unlikely to lose.

14 WEDNESDAY   *Moon Age Day 24 Moon Sign Scorpio*

The Moon now enters the sign of Scorpio, which heralds that part of the month known as the lunar low. This is because Scorpio is your opposite zodiac sign and the result is that you have less energy and need more time to yourself than might sometimes be the case. Don't take on anything too strenuous for now and relax.

15 THURSDAY
Moon Age Day 25 Moon Sign Scorpio

You will still not be firing on all cylinders so don't be afraid to rely on others in order to get something important done. Not everyone seems to have your best interests at heart right now, but your perspectives are not exactly what they might be. Could it be that you are making more out of certain situations than they really deserve?

16 FRIDAY
Moon Age Day 26 Moon Sign Scorpio

This would be a particularly good time to get rid of old attachments that are no longer any use to you. This trend does not really relate to people but rather things. Taurus is inclined to collect together all sorts of trappings that really only slow you down in the end. A tidier and leaner sort of life would suit you better in 2015.

17 SATURDAY
Moon Age Day 27 Moon Sign Sagittarius

Material issues can be both difficult to deal with and rather expensive under present trends. If you stop and think, you should soon realise that the most important gifts in your life at the moment don't cost you anything at all. Be confident that friends will come good for you when it matters the most.

18 SUNDAY
Moon Age Day 28 Moon Sign Sagittarius

Today should be favourable for intimate relationships and for making progress in romantic attachments. Although you will still be working hard in a practical sense, it is the deeper qualities of your nature that predominate. Letting someone know how you really feel about him or her will be quite easy.

19 MONDAY
Moon Age Day 29 Moon Sign Capricorn

If you are feeling preoccupied with personal or emotional issues right now, you could miss good social possibilities. If your partner is quiet or family members are reacting in a rather strange way, give them space and time. Meanwhile, you can mix with friends who make fewer demands on you. Cultivate a light and breezy attitude.

20 TUESDAY   *Moon Age Day 0 Moon Sign Capricorn*

This is not a time to be weighed down by mundane issues, but rather a period during which you need to ring the changes as much as possible. You tend to graze the meadows of life at present rather than worrying yourself about what makes the grass grow. But Taurus is a natural worrier, so don't be afraid of such interludes.

21 WEDNESDAY   *Moon Age Day 1 Moon Sign Aquarius*

Professionally, you seem to be on the up and up right now. At the same time, you show a great need for change and diversity. This is a good time to make a good impression, wherever you choose to put yourself.

22 THURSDAY ☿ *Moon Age Day 2 Moon Sign Aquarius*

It would be a shame if you were to underestimate your present strengths. You are far stronger than you realise, physically and mentally, and you have such a good attitude to life at present that you can achieve almost anything. All that is required is greater self-belief, together with a little timely help.

23 FRIDAY ☿ *Moon Age Day 3 Moon Sign Pisces*

You can now afford to be much more goal-oriented than would often be the case for a Taurus subject. Use your organisational skills while they are at their peak and you'll achieve your objectives. For all this you can thank the Sun, which now occupies your solar tenth house.

24 SATURDAY ☿ *Moon Age Day 4 Moon Sign Pisces*

Use the weekend to travel to new and previously unexplored places and do everything you can to stimulate the deeper side of your nature. You are intelligent and shrewd, but somewhat lacking in stimulation at the moment. It is your attitude and the arrangements that you make now that will bring this to you.

25 SUNDAY ☿ *Moon Age Day 5 Moon Sign Aries*

Take every chance to get out and about, because today you could meet people who will be of real use to you in the future, as well as individuals who simply interest you. Don't concentrate on the same old things; for now, you will be far better off taking a fairly superficial attitude when possible.

26 MONDAY ☿ *Moon Age Day 6 Moon Sign Aries*

There is probably no inherent fear at the moment when it comes to taking quite significant risks. This is because you are sure of yourself and are also inspired by other people who give you greater confidence. The chances of you being let down around now are quite small.

27 TUESDAY ☿ *Moon Age Day 7 Moon Sign Taurus*

Practical affairs become easier to control, though it is also clear that with the Moon in Taurus you will also want to do everything you can to have fun. This is likely to be a time during which you would be happy to be out and about with your friends. When it comes to painting the town red, you will have the biggest brush of all.

28 WEDNESDAY ☿ *Moon Age Day 8 Moon Sign Taurus*

This is an ideal time to set out on a few new projects that have been at the back of your mind for a while. Getting others to do your bidding should be very easy indeed and there will be no lack of positive indications that you are going in the right direction. In a social sense, things begin to sing for you.

29 THURSDAY ☿ *Moon Age Day 9 Moon Sign Gemini*

Current trends suggest that you will thrive on doing several different tasks at the same time and won't have too much difficulty making sure that they are all done well. The day could bring new opportunities in your love life and you will find it easy to utter the right words of love that have someone special melting.

30 FRIDAY ☿ *Moon Age Day 10 Moon Sign Gemini*

You could have a significant part to play in your own career success today, although not by actually doing anything. Rather you are thinking ahead, planning and determining what attitude and actions to adopt. There is still scope and a great need for personal satisfaction that has nothing to do with practicalities.

31 SATURDAY ☿ *Moon Age Day 11 Moon Sign Gemini*

There are likely to be conflicts of interest around at the moment. It won't be at all easy to get what you want from life, whilst at the same time fulfilling what you see as your obligations towards others. Be careful when making new investments, because something that looks like a real bargain could turn out to be anything but.

February

2015

1 SUNDAY ☿ *Moon Age Day 12 Moon Sign Cancer*

Although you are slightly reluctant now in a social sense, you can rely on the actions and ideas of others to get you out of yourself when it matters the most. You could easily be thinking too deeply about certain issues and would be far better off grazing possibilities at the moment rather than getting too involved in anything specific.

2 MONDAY ☿ *Moon Age Day 13 Moon Sign Cancer*

Work and professional issues generally should continue to work out well for you today and if you apply your powers of concentration, you should get on well. Once responsibilities are out of the way, there is a quieter side within your nature and it might do you good to spend some quiet time alone.

3 TUESDAY ☿ *Moon Age Day 14 Moon Sign Leo*

This is a favourable time for acting on sound practical ideas, rather than shouting about things or making any sort of fuss. Simply get on and see things through to their obvious conclusions – at least obvious as far as you are concerned. It might be necessary to explain your strategies to others.

4 WEDNESDAY ☿ *Moon Age Day 15 Moon Sign Leo*

There is much to be said for capitalising on today's stimulation, but without worrying about furthering your own intentions. You can't expect to get on well with everyone at the moment and might find that you are particularly frustrated with those people who are inclined to criticise but won't get off their bottoms to make life any better.

80

5 THURSDAY ☿ *Moon Age Day 16 Moon Sign Leo*

It might seem as though you are making limited progress, professionally. In reality, though, there is a good chance that you are doing better than you think and you could notice some positive input today from family members. All the same, life could seem a little nebulous so just relax and enjoy the break.

6 FRIDAY ☿ *Moon Age Day 17 Moon Sign Virgo*

This would be a good time to work with others and to make the most of new opportunities that are definitely on the horizon. Even though you have plenty to do and not all that much time to fit everything in, it could be a mistake to rush your fences. Romance could come knocking on your door around now.

7 SATURDAY ☿ *Moon Age Day 18 Moon Sign Virgo*

You have a close bond with friends and now could be a good time to make the weekend special, not just for yourself but also for those to whom you are personally attached. Your thoughts remain quite complex and there seem to be more questions than answers. A shopping spree could lighten the load.

8 SUNDAY ☿ *Moon Age Day 19 Moon Sign Libra*

Don't get too tied up with details when it comes to romance but simply let people know how you feel. It could be that certain individuals are living an even more complicated life than you are at present and at least you will be able to steer them in the right direction. Don't be too quick to criticise people in a social environment.

9 MONDAY ☿ *Moon Age Day 20 Moon Sign Libra*

Your argumentative nature could be slightly stimulated at present and that means having to be somewhat careful in the way you approach others, especially relatives. Make the best of things today by mixing more freely with friends than with family members.

10 TUESDAY ☿ *Moon Age Day 21 Moon Sign Libra*

In a career sense life can be challenging but at least it offers you plenty to think about, together with a tendency to be right on the ball where your assumptions are concerned. In every facet of life, others will marvel at your ability to get things right first time and they might even accuse you of being a bit weird in this regard!

11 WEDNESDAY ☿ *Moon Age Day 22 Moon Sign Scorpio*

Let others take the strain today. This isn't likely to be your luckiest period of the month and neither will you be overflowing with energy and confidence. Instead, concentrate on thinking up your moves for the future. If you adopt the right attitude, you can be quite content despite the lunar low.

12 THURSDAY ☿ *Moon Age Day 23 Moon Sign Scorpio*

It looks as though you will spend a good part of today doing what others want, rather than going your own way. That's par for the course for the moment, but it's a temporary state of affairs. Actually, it could even turn out to be good to go with the flow and there is a chance that you will have some genuine fun.

13 FRIDAY ☿ *Moon Age Day 24 Moon Sign Sagittarius*

Whilst you are particularly assertive in your dealings with others, there remains a slight element of doubt in your own mind. Beware, though of showing this to the world at large, because you will get on much better if people see that you are positive and sure of yourself. Romance looks good under present trends.

14 SATURDAY *Moon Age Day 25 Moon Sign Sagittarius*

Your interests are best served today by simply following your own path. Don't deviate simply to please the sensibilities of people who haven't really any idea what either they or you should be doing. There are some possible romantic gains later in the day and friends will prove to be especially important when it comes to planning ahead for fun or travel.

15 SUNDAY · *Moon Age Day 26 Moon Sign Capricorn*

Be aware that all might not be rosy in your social affairs at this time. Friendships could be prone to conflict, so take care because it would be all too easy to upset someone without even trying. On the plus side, you can now get what you want from life and that's a definite improvement.

16 MONDAY · *Moon Age Day 27 Moon Sign Capricorn*

There is a strongly competitive element about Taurus at the moment and it is clear that you won't give in on anything once you have set your mind to it. Be warned, though, that there are some individuals around who are just as anxious to win as you are. It looks as though the scene is set for some interesting and rewarding competitions.

17 TUESDAY · *Moon Age Day 28 Moon Sign Aquarius*

Motivation is clearly the key to success at the moment, which is why you won't get a lot done if you keep taking on jobs you hate. Unsavoury tasks should be shared out fairly and there is no reason why you should always be at the front of the queue. Prompt someone else into taking a turn.

18 WEDNESDAY · *Moon Age Day 29 Moon Sign Aquarius*

Try to widen your horizons and set out to make this a time to remember. There are plenty of people around who would be more than willing to join in the fun. When Taurus is on form you are the most charming and entertaining company around, and you certainly can show yourself to be energetic under present planetary trends.

19 THURSDAY · *Moon Age Day 0 Moon Sign Pisces*

This would be a great time to travel and although the weather is unlikely to be up to much in Britain, there is a great big world out there that Taurus loves to explore. However, if foreign shores are impossible at the moment find somewhere to go that at least feels like being in the sunshine.

20 FRIDAY   *Moon Age Day 1   Moon Sign Pisces*

Being well organised and by getting others to work along lines you know to be sensible and productive is key to success at work today. You possess good powers of persuasion and a very positive psychological approach that seems to be infectious. Not everyone is on your side now, but most will be when it really matters.

21 SATURDAY   *Moon Age Day 2   Moon Sign Aries*

Expect family matters to be high on your list of priorities. Maybe family members are demanding your attention or it could be that you are supporting someone who is going through a slightly difficult period. Whatever you are doing, try to maintain a cheerful attitude and your infectious sense of humour.

22 SUNDAY   *Moon Age Day 3   Moon Sign Aries*

Take advantage of friends who are both supportive and stimulating at this time and relax a little, whilst they take some of the strain in potentially difficult situations. Life can be a breeze for those of you who are willing to take a back seat, but of course Taurus hates to let go of the reins and this can be a slight problem.

23 MONDAY   *Moon Age Day 4   Moon Sign Aries*

Routines are not for you at any stage during this week, which is why you will be anxious to ring the changes and to get some variety into your life. There are still moments during which you are looking deep inside yourself, but these represent only short interludes, brought about by a number of trends.

24 TUESDAY   *Moon Age Day 5   Moon Sign Taurus*

The general level of your luck is likely to be high and that means you can afford to back your hunches to a much greater extent than usual. People will be happy to fall in line with your plans, which makes life easier and more enjoyable. Your magnetic personality will draw people to you.

25 WEDNESDAY   *Moon Age Day 6 Moon Sign Taurus*

Most personal pursuits are now likely to be positively highlighted and there isn't much doubt that you will be anxious to get ahead. In almost every way your mind is now much clearer and more inventive than was the case only a few days ago and the lunar high offers you the chance to make the very best of impressions on others.

26 THURSDAY   *Moon Age Day 7 Moon Sign Gemini*

When it comes to practical efforts you get by with a combination of common sense and intuition. Towards the end of the week, you could find life speeding up and you will be quite happy to get back to the generally progressive attitude you have had through most of February. Someone could surprise you with a change of attitude.

27 FRIDAY   *Moon Age Day 8 Moon Sign Gemini*

You now have the chance to apply your imaginative ideas to practical situations and once again you will be in a very good position to feather your own nest. At the same time, you can assist a friend who has not been so lucky of late and as always you show that innate sensitivity that definitely sets you aside from the mainstream.

28 SATURDAY   *Moon Age Day 9 Moon Sign Cancer*

This is likely to be a forward-looking period in a professional sense. There could be so many offers on the table that you are spoiled for choice and won't know what to turn down. Yet decisions will have to be made, so turn to a good friend or colleague for advice if you can't work things out for yourself.

March

2015

1 SUNDAY
Moon Age Day 10 Moon Sign Cancer

Now you have a good ability for sustained work and can do almost anything necessary to get on top of situations. You will be full of energy and can apply yourself to any number of tasks. All the same, you need to take some time out to do whatever takes your fancy.

2 MONDAY
Moon Age Day 11 Moon Sign Leo

Ordinary routines can seem like a sort of drudgery and there isn't much doubt that you work at your best now when you can choose for yourself. There is no reason why you should have to tackle all the boring jobs yourself, so learn to delegate. When you allow yourself the time, your mind soars like an eagle.

3 TUESDAY
Moon Age Day 12 Moon Sign Leo

Today you can get the right support from the right people if you keep your eyes open and take advantage of the planetary trends. Don't get too tied down with those Taurean routines. Instead, remain flexible and leave time to do things that come along as a pleasant surprise.

4 WEDNESDAY
Moon Age Day 13 Moon Sign Leo

Things do tend to go better in pairs for you today and particularly so when it comes to everyday considerations. Once the toil is out of the way, you might still decide that you need company and will then turn to your friends. Taurus is not especially family orientated for the moment, but that situation changes closer to the weekend.

5 THURSDAY
Moon Age Day 14 Moon Sign Virgo

It is unconventional answers that best match the questions life is asking and there is little doubt that Taurus is particularly original at the moment. You can get most of what you want today simply by tuning your mind to the right frequency and very few people will stand in your way. At least one little victory is more or less certain.

6 FRIDAY
Moon Age Day 15 Moon Sign Virgo

Whilst your social life seems to be on a roll, you will also find more time to concentrate on family and those people you live with. You might not get a great deal done today that can be said to be specifically practical, but that doesn't matter because you are likely to be having a really good time.

7 SATURDAY
Moon Age Day 16 Moon Sign Libra

There are many diverse issues around today and you won't have to work very hard to make life interesting because it manages that of its own accord. Be prepared for some setbacks in practical matters, but you can use your natural resourcefulness to get around them.

8 SUNDAY
Moon Age Day 17 Moon Sign Libra

Look out for intimate encounters today and use them to help to put a new perspective on old issues. Signs are good for your progressive attitude so get going with new plans and be willing to take on board the alternative strategies of colleagues if you know instinctively that they have a strong chance of being successful.

9 MONDAY
Moon Age Day 18 Moon Sign Libra

You are a naturally deep thinker and should be looking very carefully at new information that comes your way around this time. Be on the lookout for opportunities to improve yourself intellectually. In amongst the necessary jobs, you need to find the time to do something that simply pleases you.

10 TUESDAY
Moon Age Day 19 Moon Sign Scorpio

The arrival of the lunar low means you will have to be prepared to give way to others under almost all circumstances today. Don't be too quick to try to take command and avoid panicking about issues that have no real importance. Someone you don't see too often could appear now with some interesting news.

11 WEDNESDAY
Moon Age Day 20 Moon Sign Scorpio

You would certainly be better off keeping a low profile today. In particular, try not to waste time on pointless family arguments. You will find the day goes much better if you play the honest broker and by the evening you should be feeling more comfortable and happy.

12 THURSDAY
Moon Age Day 21 Moon Sign Sagittarius

Be relentless in your quest to follow your own path, even if this means having to disagree with people close to you. Disagreement doesn't have to mean argument and you can find ways to get your point of view across without it descending into a row. Taurus is now about as diplomatic as it ever gets.

13 FRIDAY
Moon Age Day 22 Moon Sign Sagittarius

From a social point of view you could be much busier now and for many Taurus subjects the weekend is likely to start early. It would do you a great deal of good to get out of doors and to enjoy what the early spring has to offer. OK, so it might still be cold, but you can easily wrap up and would benefit from some fresh air.

14 SATURDAY
Moon Age Day 23 Moon Sign Sagittarius

A change can be as good as a rest and that certainly seems to apply to Taurus today. Get out of the house and do something completely different. Things work out best when you are in the company of friends, or maybe when you can spend a few hours with your partner. The sights and sounds of the big, wide world will be appealing.

15 SUNDAY *Moon Age Day 24 Moon Sign Capricorn*

You should find yourself in an idealistic frame of mind this Sunday and won't take no for an answer when it comes to achieving some of your most longed-for objectives for the sake of other people. Your generosity knows no bounds and you show yourself to be inspirational in your approach to those around you.

16 MONDAY *Moon Age Day 25 Moon Sign Capricorn*

The impact that others have on you is quite strong at this time and it is clear that you are making the most favourable impression imaginable. This is not to suggest that everyone takes to you and there will be people who are difficult to deal with. This is a favourable time for romance.

17 TUESDAY *Moon Age Day 26 Moon Sign Aquarius*

Whilst you are thinking quickly thinking at the moment, you could be forced into the company of people who are much slower on the uptake. This could prove to be rather frustrating and you are going to have to display that important Taurean patience in order to deal with the situation. Friends prove themselves to be loyal.

18 WEDNESDAY *Moon Age Day 27 Moon Sign Aquarius*

A good day is in store during which positive actions on your part can save you a great deal of time later. Stay away from anything tedious or boring and, if possible, get out into the good fresh air. The first stirrings of spring are at hand and Taurus appreciates this fact better than anyone.

19 THURSDAY *Moon Age Day 28 Moon Sign Pisces*

The presence of Mars, a fairly slow-moving planet could make you feel assertive or even argumentative This is a phase that could be around for a while, but it is only likely to show itself in situations where other people are trying to put one over on you – or at least when you think they are!

20 FRIDAY

Moon Age Day 0 Moon Sign Pisces

Make the most of improvements today to relate to others intellectually and learn from them about subjects that have been at the back of your mind. Being willing to change your mind is important and fortunately some of the intransigence of Taurus is likely to be taking a holiday compared to yesterday. The more flexible you are, the greater your potential.

21 SATURDAY

Moon Age Day 1 Moon Sign Aries

You will be in your element today when you find yourself involved in heady debates or in situations that demand that you thinking quickly. Intuitive and perceptive, you are able to twist and turn with the subject matter at hand and won't lose any chance to tell it how it is. Whether others will agree remains to be seen.

22 SUNDAY

Moon Age Day 2 Moon Sign Aries

Getting what you really want from life can be a slight struggle for the moment, mainly because you are quieter by nature right now and less able to push yourself forward. This is a temporary state of affairs, brought about by the Moon passing through your solar twelfth house. Others will find you to be particularly understanding.

23 MONDAY

Moon Age Day 3 Moon Sign Taurus

Right now you clearly have the knack for success and the lunar high proves to be a very positive driving force. You are ready to work hard to achieve your objectives and won't be held back by the negative responses of some of your colleagues and friends. On the contrary, you can even turn their pessimism to your advantage.

24 TUESDAY

Moon Age Day 4 Moon Sign Taurus

You are still on a roll and show yourself to be equal to just about any task you choose to take on. There are gains to be made on the financial front and it looks as though you have what it takes to win a real coup in the sphere of romance. Taurus people who have been looking for a new love should keep their eyes open.

25 WEDNESDAY *Moon Age Day 5 Moon Sign Gemini*

Conflict could be the order of the day today. This could come about partly because of the attitude of colleagues or friends, but also because you are in such a forceful frame of mind. On specific occasions it can be like an irresistible force meeting an immovable object – and there is nobody more stubborn than Taurus.

26 THURSDAY *Moon Age Day 6 Moon Sign Gemini*

Opportunities are on the way for making new friendships, and you are at your most sociable for March. Spring is showing itself more every day and that suits you fine because you are a spring-born individual yourself. You should be generally cheerful and find ways to lift the spirits of friends.

27 FRIDAY *Moon Age Day 7 Moon Sign Cancer*

You are now likely to be positive in your attitude, but even so you might feel that you have to please too many people and that you would rather simply do what suits you. There is nothing wrong with feeling this way, except fact that you have a very active conscience and might feel guilty if you feel you have been selfish.

28 SATURDAY *Moon Age Day 8 Moon Sign Cancer*

Your thoughts and moods fluctuate somewhat this weekend and you could discover that you are able to overcome past problems simply by looking at them in a new and revolutionary way. A break from the ordinary is called for in your social and personal life, too. The more you surprise others, the greater your personal satisfaction will be.

29 SUNDAY *Moon Age Day 9 Moon Sign Cancer*

Learning to relax and to be content with your lot is your homework for this Sunday. Don't get anxious, particularly about situations you cannot possibility alter. If you do get a little depressed by anything, cast your gaze towards those who have much greater problems but who are dealing with them cheerfully and well.

30 MONDAY   *Moon Age Day 10 Moon Sign Leo*

Think less about what you can take from either friendships or associations with colleagues and instead mull over what you can offer. It's a fact of life at the moment that the more you give, the greater will be your own satisfaction and success. New social encounters could turn into important friendships.

31 TUESDAY   *Moon Age Day 11 Moon Sign Leo*

You show yourself to be a giving person this week, because most of what you do is undertaken for those around you. It's a funny thing, but the more you offer, the greater are the gifts that come your way. No zodiac sign typifies this more than yours. Socially, you will be great fun to have around throughout the day.

April

2015

1 WEDNESDAY
Moon Age Day 12 Moon Sign Virgo

Things are likely to be going your way, at least during the first part of the day. By the time the afternoon comes along there could be one or two little complications to deal with but nothing that will get in your way for very long. In the main you are able to put a definite full stop to tasks that have been around for quite some time.

2 THURSDAY
Moon Age Day 13 Moon Sign Virgo

Communication is the watchword today. Don't miss out on important news that is doing the rounds at the moment. By keeping your ear to the ground today you could get ahead in a project that will see you making significant progress in your life. You are less likely to be argumentative and you really do want to know how others feel and to learn what they know.

3 FRIDAY
Moon Age Day 14 Moon Sign Virgo

Recent events have been running at a fast pace, but are likely to slow somewhat for the next few days. This is not to suggest that life is going to become dull or lack any real interest. However, if you let your thoughts turn more to matters of the home and family your concentration will be better.

4 SATURDAY
Moon Age Day 15 Moon Sign Libra

The more leisure and pleasure you can get into your life at this stage of the week, the better you will feel about things generally. It is important that you do not allow yourself to get bogged down with pointless jobs and you really do need to feel important at this stage. Routines are definitely for the birds at the moment.

5 SUNDAY
Moon Age Day 16 Moon Sign Libra

Relationships are so important to you today that you will go to almost any lengths to strengthen them and to make you feel content with your lot. Romance pops into your life, perhaps when you least expect it, and you are really on the ball when it comes to finding those very special words of love that can make all the difference.

6 MONDAY
Moon Age Day 17 Moon Sign Scorpio

As today gets under way your spirits might be lower than they have been for the last few days. This is because the lunar low is around and it is likely to make you feel as though you are climbing a sizeable mountain, especially at work. Socially, you remain in good spirits, but you might actively choose to spend some time alone.

7 TUESDAY
Moon Age Day 18 Moon Sign Scorpio

Don't expect miracles from plans and objectives today. Be prepared to settle for second best or, maybe better still, avoid doing more than you have to. Not everyone around you seems to be equally helpful today and even your partner or sweetheart might be causing a few problems. Tomorrow should be better.

8 WEDNESDAY
Moon Age Day 19 Moon Sign Scorpio

There could still be one or two individuals around today who don't seem to know what they are doing and who will constantly call upon your ability to sort things out. This won't really bother you at all, because you long to feel needed and can be certain to come up with the right answers, no matter what.

9 THURSDAY
Moon Age Day 20 Moon Sign Sagittarius

One-to-one relationships need some special attention today. There could be arguments within the family and even though you are not the one promoting them, you could still find that you are involved. The only way to avoid confrontation is to back down and that is something that Taurus sometimes finds hard to do.

10 FRIDAY
Moon Age Day 21 Moon Sign Sagittarius

Increased social activity can be expected and your intellectual curiosity seems to be aroused at every turn. Make sure you get some fresh air today because this would not be a good time for sitting around and doing nothing. Blow away the cobwebs with a trip out. If it's raining, you can wear a coat! Friends should be very funny and good company today.

11 SATURDAY
Moon Age Day 22 Moon Sign Capricorn

This would be another good day to take a trip or to plan something very different and exotic. What won't suit you at all is to follow the same old routines all day long. You need something to look forward to, while at the same time discovering new ways to get your mind working at full stretch. Romance looks promising today.

12 SUNDAY
Moon Age Day 23 Moon Sign Capricorn

Getting into heated debates with anyone today could prove counterproductive. It would be far better to bite your tongue than to end up arguing about something that probably isn't very important in any case. If you do allow yourself to get involved in matters that are not really within your province, you will regret it later.

13 MONDAY
Moon Age Day 24 Moon Sign Aquarius

Getting along with everyone you meet is not going to be the easiest thing in the world, because there are a few individuals around now who can annoy you simply by being alive. All Taurus people have their likes and dislikes, and at the moment you are coming face to face with many of yours. Stay patient and don't react if provoked.

14 TUESDAY
Moon Age Day 25 Moon Sign Aquarius

There isn't much that you are being outspoken today – in fact there are times when you really ought to bite your tongue. Such situations usually come about when Taurus is defending someone else and that is likely to be the scenario now. Just make certain you know your facts before really having a go at anyone.

15 WEDNESDAY
Moon Age Day 26 Moon Sign Pisces

Right now you should be taking time off from ordinary routines so that you can find moments for deep insights into life as a whole and where it is presently leading you. A few minor alterations might be necessary, and though these don't seem like much they can have a tremendous bearing on your longer term future.

16 THURSDAY
Moon Age Day 27 Moon Sign Pisces

It isn't so much what it is going on in front of your face that you find so appealing today, but rather what is happening behind the scenes. It's clear that your curiosity is aroused and that you will not stop moving stones just to see what is under them. Just be careful that you don't annoy anyone else by appearing to be nosey.

17 FRIDAY
Moon Age Day 28 Moon Sign Aries

Relax and trust that most matters will turn out well in the long run. This is not a time to exhibit undue anxiety, if only because you will telegraph the fact to others and make them worry, too. In any case, most of what you are anxious about is either unimportant or will soon disappear like the morning mist.

18 SATURDAY
Moon Age Day 29 Moon Sign Aries

There are issues to deal with today and these ought to be sorted out ahead of the lunar high that comes along tomorrow. You won't mind a little routine for the moment and have what it takes to sort out situations, even if to others they look like a tangled ball of string. Patience is one of your best virtues and it shows now.

19 SUNDAY
Moon Age Day 0 Moon Sign Taurus

The lunar high returns and brings with it a sudden surge in energy and a great desire to get things done. New projects are in store and you can break down barriers from the past in order to get what you want from life. Bringing others round to your point of view should be child's play under present astrological trends.

20 MONDAY
Moon Age Day 1 Moon Sign Taurus

This would be a really good time to consolidate recent gains and also to show just how capable you are. The lunar high makes you luckier than usual and should ensure that you are able to put just the right amount of effort into anything you undertake. As a result, this ought to be a fascinating and useful sort of day.

21 TUESDAY
Moon Age Day 2 Moon Sign Gemini

Mental talents and the ability to communicate your ideas and opinions to others are definitely strong at the moment. This could be a crackerjack of a day, particularly on the social front. Do your best to mix as much as possible, rather than getting tied down by domestic responsibilities.

22 WEDNESDAY
Moon Age Day 3 Moon Sign Gemini

Many issues could be resolved now, if you could only summon up the energy to think about them. Things are the way they are for the moment and you will only become frustrated if you try to alter anything significant right now. By tomorrow you are much more dynamic, but for the moment you should relax and float.

23 THURSDAY
Moon Age Day 4 Moon Sign Gemini

The planetary focus is now specifically on personal interests and abilities. It might seem selfish, but it isn't. Unless you get things running the way you know they should, you won't have either the time or the money to share with those you love. This is one of those times when Taurus is very practical indeed.

24 FRIDAY
Moon Age Day 5 Moon Sign Cancer

This can be one of the most rewarding periods of the month in a social sense, so as April is growing older, you become ever more committed to enjoyment with friends. Work might seem to be getting in the way, but there are opportunities for you to mix business with pleasure. It's simply a case of thinking things through.

25 SATURDAY
Moon Age Day 6 Moon Sign Cancer

Communication increases as Saturday dawns and you will be talking freely to just about anyone you come across now. You will be happy to go on a shopping spree, or even to have a trip out with your partner or a friend. What wouldn't be too good today would be to stick around usual places, doing the same old things.

26 SUNDAY
Moon Age Day 7 Moon Sign Leo

It ought to be a piece of cake getting relatives and friends to do things for you at the moment. Such are your powers of persuasion that you could sell fridges to the Inuit. When it comes to financial matters, it might be best to defer to someone who has more experience of a very particular situation than you do yourself.

27 MONDAY
Moon Age Day 8 Moon Sign Leo

This is a time when you should be looking at far-reaching plans and working out how to make them work much earlier than you might previously have expected. You remain very optimistic, know what you want from life and can easily get the people on board who will be in the best possible position to help you out.

28 TUESDAY
Moon Age Day 9 Moon Sign Leo

It might be necessary to weigh the balance between work and home around now, so if the opportunity presents itself, take a few moments to be on your own and to think. There will be distractions about, but these will not prevent you from finding a little corner where you can meditate in peace.

29 WEDNESDAY
Moon Age Day 10 Moon Sign Virgo

Getting personal recognition isn't too important to you today. What matters more is making certain that things are done efficiently and properly. It will be easy to become annoyed with individuals who won't do what you tell them or people who seem determined to throw a spanner in the works simply to be mischievous.

30 THURSDAY
Moon Age Day 11 Moon Sign Virgo

Apply a little self-discipline today. In your dealings with others it is important to sort out the wheat from the chaff. In a practical sense you should only throw in your lot with those who have proved themselves to be reliable and capable. Co-operation is very important now, but so is careful selection before you commit yourself.

May

2015

1 FRIDAY
Moon Age Day 12 Moon Sign Libra

Today could prove to be slightly trying as far as personal relationships are concerned. It seems as though many situations are custom-designed to get on your wrong side, though the problem probably lies within our attitude rather than anywhere else. A little more patience and some genuine diplomacy might help.

2 SATURDAY
Moon Age Day 13 Moon Sign Libra

There are good friends around you at the moment and it is likely to be towards them that you turn for advice or practical help at present. In family matters, you will tend to be thoughtful and looking for ways to lend a hand to someone who is too proud to ask for your assistance. A little psychology is called for.

3 SUNDAY
Moon Age Day 14 Moon Sign Libra

You can find great pleasure in social moments and when you are working hard to please your partner or sweetheart. There are slightly more wearing moments today, particularly if you committed to following a course of action at home that you know to be little more than a waste of time. Taurus is inclined to speak out under present trends.

4 MONDAY
Moon Age Day 15 Moon Sign Scorpio

A brief respite is not only advisable, but may also prove to be quite inevitable today. The attitudes of family members are likely to be difficult to understand and it would be better to avoid getting involved in deep discussions that seem to have no real purpose. Although you are quite political at present, this subject, too, should be avoided.

100

5 TUESDAY
Moon Age Day 16 Moon Sign Scorpio

Today it is a question of seeking out some light relief where you can. Don't take yourself or anyone else too seriously and be willing to laugh at your own ineptitude. If you start to look too deeply into life and its peculiarities you could be in for a few less than favourable experiences. Be a browser for day or two and avoid being serious.

6 WEDNESDAY
Moon Age Day 17 Moon Sign Sagittarius

Although you will be very quick to push your ideas forward at the moment, it might be better to be more circumspect for a while. What your schemes need is just a little refinement and that won't be possible once they are public property. What you don't want is someone to improve your ideas and then cast them as their own.

7 THURSDAY
Moon Age Day 18 Moon Sign Sagittarius

Use the present period in order to rise to the many career issues that are likely to be on your mind just at the moment. At the same time you seem to be very busy with ideas that are going to have a great bearing on your home life. Not everyone will be equally helpful at the moment, but it's a fair bet you know how to get what you need.

8 FRIDAY
Moon Age Day 19 Moon Sign Capricorn

You may have a definite desire to please yourself today and there's nothing wrong with that, just as long as you don't ignore those people who are doing their best to make you take notice of them. A little self-indulgence will allow you to catch up on all those half-ideas that have yet to get to the forefront of your mind.

9 SATURDAY
Moon Age Day 20 Moon Sign Capricorn

You maintain a generally bright and breezy attitude to life and should be more than happy to try something new on a number of different occasions at the moment. Routines could be something of a bind and you will be doing all you can to avoid them if at all possible. Listen to your intuition, which is strong at present.

10 SUNDAY   *Moon Age Day 21 Moon Sign Aquarius*

This is a good day to stay at home, so fill your Sunday with domestic matters. Make the most of the opportunity to sort out a few issues that could have been festering below the surface. People air their opinions and you can, too.

11 MONDAY   *Moon Age Day 22 Moon Sign Aquarius*

Good things are now likely to happen from a social point of view and it looks as though you are in for a day of significant events. Some of these come like a bolt from the blue and you will need to be open to any sort of input today. This would be a great time to go out and seek a bargain, especially something for your home.

12 TUESDAY   *Moon Age Day 23 Moon Sign Aquarius*

Your natural intuition is extremely strong around now and so if that little voice at the back of your mind is telling you something, you really ought to pay attention. For once your gut reactions are worth more to you than that famous Taurean common sense. Look out for a few surprises and the occasional peculiar or even weird happening.

13 WEDNESDAY   *Moon Age Day 24 Moon Sign Pisces*

You could end up in two minds about a plethora of situations today, because you are simply not half as sure of yourself as you sometimes are. Acting on impulse might not be your thing, but this is a favourable time to do just that. Romantic partners are hard to understand, but even so they can offer some fascinating insights.

14 THURSDAY   *Moon Age Day 25 Moon Sign Pisces*

Things could be on the up today. It is possible that you will find yourself better off than you were a week or two ago. Relationships should be running smoothly and you could have the opportunity today to broach a ticklish subject and get away with it.

15 FRIDAY
Moon Age Day 26 Moon Sign Aries

Professional matters tend to be positively highlighted under current trends, but that doesn't mean you will be ignoring your personal life. On the contrary, you are filled with words and expressions that are custom-made to please your partner. Although you may not be much of a gambler, you probably could afford to take the odd calculated risk now.

16 SATURDAY
Moon Age Day 27 Moon Sign Aries

Other people have a beneficial influence on your life at the moment. That is part of the reason why you are showing yourself to be a team player around this time. Social gatherings should appeal and there will be opportunities to shine in a way that Taurus sometimes does. Don't be too fussy about details during the weekend.

17 SUNDAY
Moon Age Day 28 Moon Sign Taurus

Money matters are favoured today, as the lunar high brings a breath of fresh air into your life in respect of new possibilities. Your social life is also likely to be extremely active and you could use your increasing popularity to give you more confidence and make advances.

18 MONDAY
Moon Age Day 0 Moon Sign Taurus

Most of your expectations can be fulfilled at the moment and you show the world what you are capable of achieving, often without a great deal of effort on your part. Although there are limits to your capabilities at the moment you will have to work very hard in order to find them. Friends should be especially approachable now.

19 TUESDAY
☿ *Moon Age Day 1 Moon Sign Gemini*

If there is one thing that is going to be noticeable today, it will be your sensitivity, which is even more pronounced than usual. This would be a good day to get half-finished jobs out of the way, especially those that require a degree of concentration. Look out for new activities beckoning towards the end of the day.

20 WEDNESDAY ☿   *Moon Age Day 2 Moon Sign Gemini*

Communication matters should still be high on your agenda. There is plenty to be gained by being on the move and by speaking out first. Taurus is inclined to be slightly reserved at times, but if you don't make yourself known now you will miss some sparkling opportunities. Explain your ideas to anyone who will listen.

21 THURSDAY ☿   *Moon Age Day 3 Moon Sign Cancer*

With plenty to keep you interested in the day-to-day, this should be one of the most settled and happy periods of the month. This is the part of the year you love the most and it works well for you because of the position of the Sun around now. Show your versatility, curiosity and a youthful enthusiasm.

22 FRIDAY ☿   *Moon Age Day 4 Moon Sign Cancer*

It's true that there is something of the butterfly about you at the moment, mainly because so many different things take your fancy and you will be flitting around from one situation to another. This is not necessarily a bad thing because as a Taurean you sometimes over-concentrate. Allow yourself the right to be somewhat fickle for now.

23 SATURDAY ☿   *Moon Age Day 5 Moon Sign Leo*

You could now be over-concerned with making the right impression. The best advice for the moment is simply to be yourself and to let others judge you accordingly. In most situations you won't be found lacking and you show a great flair when it comes to brightening up your environment, either at work or later when you are at home.

24 SUNDAY ☿   *Moon Age Day 6 Moon Sign Leo*

Play your cards right and this could be a day of considerable profit. Not all of the gains on offer are financial in nature, because there can be profit in happiness, a fact that is rarely lost on Taurus. You might be a bit over fussy and it's true that you want to have everything just so, but that's part of the hallmark of your zodiac sign.

25 MONDAY ☿ *Moon Age Day 7 Moon Sign Leo*

Try to be as original as you can today and let other people know that there is nothing run-of-the-mill about you. The more you make yourself known, the better are the chances that you will enlist the support that is presently so vital to many of your enterprises. The charitable side of your nature is showing more than ever, too.

26 TUESDAY ☿ *Moon Age Day 8 Moon Sign Virgo*

Be prepared for an emotionally challenging time, probably because those closest to you, and especially your partner, are not behaving in quite the way you might expect. Much of this has to do with your present state of mind. You are adaptable and so can soon get used to changes within your environment.

27 WEDNESDAY ☿ *Moon Age Day 9 Moon Sign Virgo*

An inspiring time of constantly expanding horizons lies before you, but there will be occasions when you need to look carefully before you proceed. That's part of what this midweek period is about. Take a few hours out and spend some time analysing your thoughts, because there are always newer and better ways to get things done.

28 THURSDAY ☿ *Moon Age Day 10 Moon Sign Libra*

There could be a feeling of urgency about getting certain tasks out of the way, but in reality you don't need to rush your fences quite so much. Under present trends, it would be far better to make sure that everything is completed in a satisfactory manner before you move on. Rushing rarely achieves anything in the world of Taurus.

29 FRIDAY ☿ *Moon Age Day 11 Moon Sign Libra*

A little soul-searching may be in order as you come to terms with elements of the past. Don't allow any over-emotional behaviour to upset your dealings with the world at large, and try to remain impartial when you are faced with the disagreements others are having. There is profit in playing the honest broker today.

30 SATURDAY ☿   *Moon Age Day 12 Moon Sign Libra*

Changeability is the key to success, which doesn't always come easy to Taurus. However, you will make better progress if you can remain adaptable. If there are things to do today that you don't like the look of, put them to one side and do what takes your fancy instead. Finding allies with whom you can be silly won't be hard!

31 SUNDAY ☿   *Moon Age Day 13 Moon Sign Scorpio*

This might not turn out to be the most satisfying day of the month for you and it is true that you do have the lunar low to contend with. It all depends on your expectations, and if you are willing to take a break and to rest a little, all should be well. Problems will only arise if you refuse to accept a slower pace.

June

2015

1 MONDAY
☿ *Moon Age Day 14 Moon Sign Scorpio*

Things are still not looking wonderful, but you are one of the most resilient people to be found throughout the length and breadth of the zodiac. In your need to find new ways to solve old problems you should be able to impress both yourself and the world at large. All in all, what happens today could prove just how ingenious you can be.

2 TUESDAY
☿ *Moon Age Day 15 Moon Sign Sagittarius*

The signs are that you will be the one in your social circle who comes up with all the good ideas and makes most of the arrangements. Not everything you have in mind will please your all your friends and it might be necessary to be just a little selective before choosing your present pals.

3 WEDNESDAY
☿ *Moon Age Day 16 Moon Sign Sagittarius*

The time is right for opting for the bright lights of the social world whenever you can. The year is advancing and you will want to make all you can out of the early summer and the opportunities it offers for new and exciting adventures. Taurus is now at its optimistic best and you will also be less fussy than is often the case.

4 THURSDAY
☿ *Moon Age Day 17 Moon Sign Sagittarius*

Teamwork matters today. If you are willing to get involved with a new group of people who seem to have the same sort of ambitions as you do, the result could eventually be electrifying. Get to grips with new technology around this time and seek some help with gadgets you don't understand. A younger family member might help.

5 FRIDAY ☿ *Moon Age Day 18 Moon Sign Capricorn*

Certain choices will prove to be extremely rewarding today, and the only difficulty lies in knowing which way to jump under any given circumstance. Rely on your intuition, which remains well honed at present. Don't be surprised if you discover you have an admirer you never suspected – but don't act astonished.

6 SATURDAY ☿ *Moon Age Day 19 Moon Sign Capricorn*

What with your ego now much stronger than would sometimes be the case, it looks as though you might need to take care regarding your partner's feelings. You are not insensitive as a rule, but there are occasions when Taurus subjects become so sure of their own opinions, they fail to register that there are other ways of seeing life.

7 SUNDAY ☿ *Moon Age Day 20 Moon Sign Aquarius*

Since domestic situations can cause you a few irritations this Sunday. Combine this with the advancing summer, and you are likely to be looking away from your home at present. Look for some excitement and if nobody else has any good ideas, think up one or two for yourself. Anything would do, as long as it's not routine.

8 MONDAY ☿ *Moon Age Day 21 Moon Sign Aquarius*

Now you seem to find it useful to throw in your lot with others. As you co-operate, it is definitely a case that the sum of the whole is greater than the parts. In other words, no matter how good your own ideas and actions may be, they are thrown into stark relief by the progress you make when two or more people are involved.

9 TUESDAY ☿ *Moon Age Day 22 Moon Sign Pisces*

There can be a few challenges around at the moment, but you are in the right frame of mind to approach these head on. Acting on impulse is possible, but it is far more likely that you will be lining up your mental weapons in order to deal with matters in your own inimitable way. Friends should be supportive, but relatives might not be.

10 WEDNESDAY ☿   *Moon Age Day 23 Moon Sign Pisces*

Keep abreast of local news and views, whilst at the same time staying in touch with national and world affairs. An informed Taurus is a more successful one, and in any case you can prove yourself to others by the sheer power of your knowledge at the moment. This stands you in good stead when advancement is offered.

11 THURSDAY ☿   *Moon Age Day 24 Moon Sign Aries*

Although there are matters about which you no nothing today, such is the quality of your nature that nobody would ever guess the fact. Using what you do know, together with those famous Taurean hunches, you can steer a careful path and impress a wealth of people on the way. Stand by for a slightly slower couple of days.

12 FRIDAY ☿   *Moon Age Day 25 Moon Sign Aries*

There are gains to be made today, but you should also register it as being a fairly quiet time, since the Moon now occupies your solar twelfth house. You need to be sure of yourself when it comes to romantic attachments, but a little variety and the ability to react according to changing circumstances is also necessary.

13 SATURDAY   *Moon Age Day 26 Moon Sign Taurus*

One of your greatest assets whilst the lunar high is around is your optimism, coupled with an insatiable desire to try as many new things as you can. The world loves to have you around and almost everyone you meet is likely to have a smile on his or her face. Professionally, socially and romantically, it looks as though you are really motoring.

14 SUNDAY   *Moon Age Day 27 Moon Sign Taurus*

You show yourself to be a larger than life character and there are certain people around who are likely to be surprised by the person you seem to be just now. Taurus people can be a little odd: on the one hand they tend to be quiet and contemplative, but on the other, when the planets line up well – look, out world!

15 MONDAY   *Moon Age Day 28 Moon Sign Gemini*

The focus now is on practical work and on your overwhelming desire not to let things slide. Colleagues may be less committed than you are and this could be a slight bone of contention. Once work is out of the way, ring the changes in some way – maybe even travel. Holidays will be beckoning for some lucky Taureans.

16 TUESDAY   *Moon Age Day 29 Moon Sign Gemini*

Now a much more decisive side to your nature begins to show. You know very well what you want from life and will have a very good idea how to get it. It is possible you will feel somewhat impatient and might not be quite as good at dealing with the emotional needs of others as might sometimes be the case.

17 WEDNESDAY   *Moon Age Day 0 Moon Sign Cancer*

You communicate well and can get most of what you want simply by asking for it. There will be absolutely no need to throw your weight about. You articulate yourself very well indeed, so finding new ways to express old ideas should be quite easy. Approach all objectives with the absolute expectation that you will succeed.

18 THURSDAY   *Moon Age Day 1 Moon Sign Cancer*

This is a favourable time for eliciting the help of other people today and you won't be short of admirers. It looks as though you will be very successful in almost anything you decide to undertake and there isn't much doubt regarding your general popularity. Perhaps best of all you might be lucky in a financial sense and can take the odd chance.

19 FRIDAY   *Moon Age Day 2 Moon Sign Cancer*

Fresh experiences will appeal to you at this time and you won't take kindly to being stuck in any sort of rut. You will fight tenaciously in order to have fresh air to breathe and new horizons to view. This applies just as much at work as it does in a social sense. Some Taureans might even be thinking about changing jobs soon.

20 SATURDAY
Moon Age Day 3 Moon Sign Leo

Today brings out the fun side of your personality and allows you to show your best face to the world at large. Under present influences, everything seems to be lining itself up in the way you would wish. Relationships look particularly secure and you make extra efforts to please family and friends.

21 SUNDAY
Moon Age Day 4 Moon Sign Leo

Although today could start fairly quietly, that almost certainly isn't the way things are going to be in the longer term. On the contrary, the present position of Mars pushes you forward again and ensures that any temporary holiday from responsibilities and effort has come to an end. You won't be sorry to be fully in gear.

22 MONDAY
Moon Age Day 5 Moon Sign Virgo

You show yourself to be very disciplined and a good worker, even if you have to look hard at first to find anything much to do. Aside from domestic chores you might have to be quite inventive and may well get a great deal of pleasure from entertaining. Long journeys are not likely today, at a time when the world comes to you.

23 TUESDAY
Moon Age Day 6 Moon Sign Virgo

Much is now tailored in your life towards practical matters and you will have so much you want to do today that it is very unlikely everything will be completed to your satisfaction. Perhaps you should try to achieve less? At least that way you can be happy with what you finish and won't end up feeling frustrated.

24 WEDNESDAY
Moon Age Day 7 Moon Sign Virgo

A friend or colleague can put you in touch with broader issues and all social contacts at the moment have an element of the weird and the wonderful. A strange period begins to open up for you, but it is going to be quite entertaining and even intriguing. Rules and regulations could easily get on your nerves.

25 THURSDAY
Moon Age Day 8 Moon Sign Libra

This could be a good day to talk to someone special and to make new attachments from what were previously only acquaintances. Under current trends, someone who thinks you are wonderful will be quite likely to tell you so. How you react to all the compliments remains to be seen. Try to do more than simply blushing.

26 FRIDAY
Moon Age Day 9 Moon Sign Libra

Independence is gradually becoming your middle name. You certainly won't take kindly to being told what to do and Taurus can be very stubborn at times. You tend to think you know best for most of the time and you will be very anxious to follow your own ideas to their conclusions.

27 SATURDAY
Moon Age Day 10 Moon Sign Scorpio

Be prepared for unavoidable and repeated delays and setbacks today and tomorrow, due to the arrival of the lunar low. Since there is very little you can do to change things, you might just as well settle down and find ways round problems. This will most likely involve getting others to work steadily on your behalf.

28 SUNDAY
Moon Age Day 11 Moon Sign Scorpio

There are obstacles, delays and frustrations, but none of these is likely to hold you up for more than a few minutes. It isn't the intensity of issues that is the problem now, but more the fact that they stop the flow of your life. This is a very temporary situation, and one that has a great deal of humour or even comedy about it.

29 MONDAY
Moon Age Day 12 Moon Sign Scorpio

Self-expression is now the key to happiness, so it is worth searching for just the right words to tell others how you feel. You won't be at all keen to get involved in anything dirty or unsavoury and would be quite willing at the moment to let others do some of the less pleasant jobs. The only problem is that they might complain about the fact.

30 TUESDAY   *Moon Age Day 13 Moon Sign Sagittarius*

Things should now go much better in terms of your interactions with loved ones. This may well be because today's trends are giving you slightly more time to please yourself and to concentrate on relationships. Try to ring the changes in a social sense, even if it is only by going somewhere different for a few hours.

July

2015

1 WEDNESDAY
Moon Age Day 14 Moon Sign Sagittarius

It seems that you will be very happy when you can do things for other people. There's nothing especially strange about this, but what is different is the fact that you may not even know the people concerned. Your mind turns to global matters and the charitable side of your nature is much enhanced by present planetary trends.

2 THURSDAY
Moon Age Day 15 Moon Sign Capricorn

While making progress and getting things done is what keeps you generally cheerful today, you will also be feeling your responsibilities to others quite keenly. Relationships in the workplace could be a little strained and you need to do all you can to get things back on to a more even keel. Your social impulses will be strong.

3 FRIDAY
Moon Age Day 16 Moon Sign Capricorn

Don't be too quick to criticise others over issues you don't understand all that well yourself. Rather than finding fault, it would be better to pitch in, co-operate and to lend a hand to sort things out. You can have a great deal of fun at the moment by pooling your resources with others and by maintaining a positive attitude.

4 SATURDAY
Moon Age Day 17 Moon Sign Aquarius

This is a favourable time for unexpected compliments to boost your ego strongly. If gadgets go wrong at home you will have to tell yourself that nothing lasts forever and shell out to replace them. Before you do, however, look around for a bargain.

5 SUNDAY
Moon Age Day 18 Moon Sign Aquarius

On the home front, try for a temporary respite from duties and demands, by getting someone else to take some of the pressure off you. Delegation is an art and it's one that you don't always understand. Under present trends, you have what it takes to trust others to do things capably and well.

6 MONDAY
Moon Age Day 19 Moon Sign Pisces

Certain issues at work are going to be demanding your attention to such an extent that you won't have all the time you would wish to spend with loved ones or friends. The problem is that even when you are not directly engaged in your professional life, it is still likely to be on your mind. Try to relax, if only for short periods.

7 TUESDAY
Moon Age Day 20 Moon Sign Pisces

You are likely to be very confident under present planetary trends and that has to be good for your every aspect of your life. Things go wrong for Taurus when it is apprehensive about both the present and the future, but you exude so much confidence at present that you also enjoy a great deal of optimism.

8 WEDNESDAY
Moon Age Day 21 Moon Sign Aries

Extended negotiations and major decisions make for an interesting, if fairly complicated, sort of Wednesday. In group situations, it is important for you to assist in reaching a consensus – a task that is often the prerogative of Taurus. For now, you remain tactful, diplomatic and capable of being an honest broker.

9 THURSDAY
Moon Age Day 22 Moon Sign Aries

There seems to be a strong social boost on the way at this stage of the week, and there are also planetary trends that will put you in touch with some fairly unusual sorts of people. Some of these will be individuals you already know, but you are also likely to be making new friends around now. Long-term plans can be addressed at present.

10 FRIDAY
Moon Age Day 23 Moon Sign Taurus

You may decide that today is right for a good deal of excitement – though in reality life itself will probably do that for you. With the Moon in your sign, you are likely to be filled with enthusiasm and will be happy to go for something newer, brighter and better. Just watch how well everyone else fits in with your plans at present.

11 SATURDAY
Moon Age Day 24 Moon Sign Taurus

This is definitely the right moment to be moving ahead in a general sense and you have what it takes to do something amazing right now. In company, you now tend to keep up a very high profile and you know what it takes to be noticed. Romantically, you exhibit all the charm necessary to knock someone for six!

12 SUNDAY
Moon Age Day 25 Moon Sign Taurus

Don't believe everything you hear today, because it is quite obvious that some of the comments that come your way are custom-designed to deceive the unwary. Fortunately, you are not one of them and it is quite clear that you remain objective and shrewd. It's also your responsibility to keep friends safe from themselves at present.

13 MONDAY
Moon Age Day 26 Moon Sign Gemini

This is a good day for mental pursuits and you certainly won't be impressed by any task that is either dirty or unsavoury. People who notice you are quiet today might interpret this as you being depressed or sulky. It is important to tell them that you are simply in a reflective frame of mind.

14 TUESDAY
Moon Age Day 27 Moon Sign Gemini

This is a time during which family issues should be working out rather well for you. Career developments look particularly good and you may well be in the offing for some sort of advancement. Since it is clear that you are being watched a good deal by your bosses right now, it would be sensible to be on your best behaviour.

15 WEDNESDAY   *Moon Age Day 28 Moon Sign Cancer*

As is often the case for Taurus, success comes from being organised and from knowing well in advance how you should behave under any given circumstance. Keep in touch with people who are in the know and plan well for some journey that is now in your mind. For the moment you may not want to travel, but you can plan.

16 THURSDAY   *Moon Age Day 0 Moon Sign Cancer*

Look out for hopeful news regarding your personal objectives, but at the same time listen very carefully to what seasoned veterans have to tell you. Older people can be very supportive under present trends. Although they might not be universally knowledgeable, what they have to tell you at the moment will be solid gold.

17 FRIDAY   *Moon Age Day 1 Moon Sign Leo*

Right now, you will be motivated most by creative challenges and will be thinking about how to get something working just right. Second best won't interest you in the slightest. Even if you end up doing the same thing time and again you will stubbornly carry on until you are totally satisfied with the results.

18 SATURDAY   *Moon Age Day 2 Moon Sign Leo*

Your affections are now easily excited and this would be a really good time to pep up your social life. There are some people around that you didn't like at all in the past, but who are now growing on you significantly. Affairs of the heart will be uppermost in your mind and there is likely to be romantic attention coming your way.

19 SUNDAY   *Moon Age Day 3 Moon Sign Leo*

You remain generally confident and will show yourself to be very capable when faced with issues you haven't necessarily dealt with before. Experience is a great thing and you can now turn yours in a number of different directions. Don't be in the least surprised if the whole world is queuing outside your door for some timely advice.

20 MONDAY
Moon Age Day 4 Moon Sign Virgo

When it comes to communication, this is a time to score significant successes. The Sun remains in a position that is good for talking and to make matters even better almost everyone seems to be listening for a change. Conversations of an inspiring nature are taking place all around you.

21 TUESDAY
Moon Age Day 5 Moon Sign Virgo

Your home might seem to be the best place to spend your time during most of today, but not because you are retreating in any way from the world at large. It is simply that you gain the greatest rewards from loved ones and that you actively want to support them all you can. Routine pressures fall away and a dreamy state takes hold.

22 WEDNESDAY
Moon Age Day 6 Moon Sign Libra

The accent is now upon your home and your family life once again. This is because the Sun has now moved into your solar fourth house, where it will remain for the next four weeks. It is quite natural at this time of year for you to spend more time reorganising your living space and also doing work of a physical nature.

23 THURSDAY
Moon Age Day 7 Moon Sign Libra

Direct your attention towards the outside world, at least in terms of friends and charitable endeavours in which you have become involved. If you have planned to push yourself physically in some way, this is the time when all of your effort and training is likely to pay off. In a practical sense, things should fall into place.

24 FRIDAY
Moon Age Day 8 Moon Sign Libra

There could be some good news coming along with regard to your future prospects and you will certainly be inclined to look ahead under present trends. What really occupies your mind around now is getting things as secure as you can in a fiscal sense. Taurus hates loose ends and this is particularly true at the moment.

25 SATURDAY
Moon Age Day 9 Moon Sign Scorpio

Put duties and demands on one side and instead of fighting against the lunar low, learn to embrace it. If you can first accept that this is not the time for advancement or progress, you will then be able to settle back and enjoy what life is offering in quieter ways. No planetary aspect or period is bad; it's all down to the way we approach them.

26 SUNDAY
Moon Age Day 10 Moon Sign Scorpio

It's time to take stock and to plan carefully for what is likely to be taking place during next week. Your general level of confidence might not be quite as high as you would wish but that doesn't mean you fail to make any movement. Most of what is happening at the moment takes place in your head.

27 MONDAY
Moon Age Day 11 Moon Sign Sagittarius

Things should be going well as far as your social life is concerned, but there could also be a few practical issues to be dealt with at this time. There is also something quite unusual and attractive about your thinking and this makes you even more popular with certain individuals. The end of a particularly awkward task is at hand.

28 TUESDAY
Moon Age Day 12 Moon Sign Sagittarius

There are a few obstacles to be overcome today, but as usual you take these in your stride and show just how resourceful you can be. Find a way to turn something that needs to be done around the home into a pleasure rather than a chore. All you need to do is to get family members involved and create a little fun on the way.

29 WEDNESDAY
Moon Age Day 13 Moon Sign Capricorn

Matters of a domestic nature should be high on your agenda for today at least. Family life is likely to be your highest priority and you actively want to spend time with those you love. If there is a contentious issue between you and your partner, a fairly serious heart-to-heart could clear the air.

30 THURSDAY *Moon Age Day 14 Moon Sign Capricorn*

The time is right for romance and you show a great ability to hog the limelight in both a romantic and a social sense. You also have a knowing knack of mixing business with pleasure, and this means you can make gains and increase your status no end. Make sure you get plenty of fresh air.

31 FRIDAY *Moon Age Day 15 Moon Sign Aquarius*

Look for new solutions to old problems. In particular, don't be afraid to seek some help from people who are genuinely in the know where money is concerned. A word of caution is necessary, though: there are plenty of people around who say they are experts, but do your research and sort out the wheat from the chaff.

⑧ August 2015

1 SATURDAY
Moon Age Day 16 Moon Sign Aquarius

This ought to be a fairly inspiring sort of day. You could gather all sorts of information, some of which will be useful in the short and medium term. You won't miss much today, and you have what it takes to turn even the most insignificant details to your advantage.

2 SUNDAY
Moon Age Day 17 Moon Sign Pisces

This is still a good time for gathering the sort of information that is going to feather your nest in the immediate future. Nothing passes you by right now and you will be particularly good at working out the genuine motivations of people close to you. Spend some time with your partner today and make a real fuss of him or her.

3 MONDAY
Moon Age Day 18 Moon Sign Pisces

Much energy is likely to be piled into your work this week and you might not have quite as much time for socialising as has been the case recently. There is assistance around if you are willing to accept it, but chances are that you are feeling quite independent. Friends should be especially warm and kind today and tomorrow.

4 TUESDAY
Moon Age Day 19 Moon Sign Aries

Look out for some completely new and unique ideas at this time. Not all of them are coming from you personally. If you keep your ears and eyes open, you will notice that other people are coming up with some very good ideas, too. Co-operation is now more likely and any sort of partnership should flourish under present planetary trends.

5 WEDNESDAY
Moon Age Day 20 Moon Sign Aries

Give yourself a pat on the back for a success that comes your way today, probably inspired by your actions some time ago. However, this is no time to be complacent, because there is plenty more to do and a wealth of possibilities in the pipeline. This will be especially true for self-employed Taurus subjects.

6 THURSDAY
Moon Age Day 21 Moon Sign Aries

A slight drop in vitality can be expected as the Moon is in your solar twelfth house, but this comes ahead of the lunar high and it does at least offer you the time you need to think carefully about the future. Beware of what you hear, because some of it may be coming from the direction of people who don't really know anything!

7 FRIDAY
Moon Age Day 22 Moon Sign Taurus

The time is right for achieving short-term goals almost instantly. Lady Luck is with you in your endeavours and you should positively enjoy being out there at the head of the field. You will have a strong faith in your own abilities and that is the most useful tool in your armoury for the moment. In terms of finances, you are now very wise.

8 SATURDAY
Moon Age Day 23 Moon Sign Taurus

You have great charm on your side right now and the lunar high offers you all the incentives you need to get ahead in a number of different ways. Send out the lunar high with a bang by getting together with your friends or relatives for a really good day away from the ordinary. Fantasy is important sometimes and can be very rewarding.

9 SUNDAY
Moon Age Day 24 Moon Sign Gemini

Be willing to emphasise what is unique about you today and don't sit in the background waiting to be noticed. There might just be a few quieter days in store, so it could be sensible to get certain jobs finished and out of the way right now. There ought to be a number of unexpected compliments coming your way at present.

10 MONDAY
Moon Age Day 25 Moon Sign Gemini

Be true to yourself and your values, but don't push issues until you force an argument. It would be far better at the moment simply to allow things to ride, rather than getting involved in situations that are unnecessary. None of this will be a problem at all if you simply go with the flow and accept what life offers.

11 TUESDAY
Moon Age Day 26 Moon Sign Cancer

There is likely to be a greater sense of purpose today, together with a feeling of lightness and frivolity. It might seem that there are conflicts as a result, but this isn't the case. The present planetary picture allows you to get exactly what you want, without having to apply much pressure to either people or situations.

12 WEDNESDAY
Moon Age Day 27 Moon Sign Cancer

Unexpected developments might open a new window in your life and you need to give all your attention to what you are doing right now. Lay down a few plans for tomorrow and expect that life will go your way. The time has come to make major decisions and to streamline your life as much as possible.

13 THURSDAY
Moon Age Day 28 Moon Sign Leo

Keeping up a high profile works wonders at this time and you should be filled with new ideas to streamline your life and throw off any redundant philosophies. Be aware of some new enterprise that is coming from the direction of a friend and join in whenever you have the chance. Social trends look especially interesting now.

14 FRIDAY
Moon Age Day 29 Moon Sign Leo

You will most likely want to end the working week with a flourish, but don't use up all your energy during the day because the evening could be especially exciting. If you have nothing specifically planned for after work, get thinking early in the day. What shows more than anything now is your rising popularity.

15 SATURDAY
Moon Age Day 0 Moon Sign Leo

Look towards cash this weekend because there are ways and means by which you can make yourself better off. Once again your ingenuity is the key, and you deal with numbers and mathematical problems quite easily at present. With finances to the fore, you might also enjoy finding new ways to spend some newly acquired money.

16 SUNDAY
Moon Age Day 1 Moon Sign Virgo

Matters close to home come under scrutiny and there is an intense focus placed on strengthening ties with your family. It might appear as though you are being forced into a corner in a professional sense, but the result is likely to be far better than you might expect. Most of this is down to your own common sense and hard work.

17 MONDAY
Moon Age Day 2 Moon Sign Virgo

In a social sense there ought to be plenty of opportunities for enjoyment this week and it all starts today. You will be chatty, forthcoming and very interesting to know. Generally speaking, this is one of the best times of the year to show others exactly what makes you tick and this is important because Taurus rarely lowers its guard.

18 TUESDAY
Moon Age Day 3 Moon Sign Libra

You might wish to break from your usual routines today and do something completely different. All the same, partnerships and other sorts of associations seem to work out very well and you will be at your best when co-operation is called for. Keep abreast of local news and views, so that you don't end up feeling out of touch.

19 WEDNESDAY
Moon Age Day 4 Moon Sign Libra

It appears you are going to be much more passionate than usual today and for this you can thank the present position of the Moon. If you feel the time is right to quit something you know has not been good for you it looks as though you will be successful. That Taurean tendency towards stubbornness can sometimes be helpful.

20 THURSDAY
Moon Age Day 5 Moon Sign Libra

A time of discrimination is at hand and you certainly won't be accepting everything you hear without question. Practical affairs are likely to be going very well and you have what it takes to break new ground and to give a good account of yourself. Others may look on in great admiration as you score one success after another.

21 FRIDAY
Moon Age Day 6 Moon Sign Scorpio

There is something about you today that proves to be especially fascinating to some of your regular contacts. Thanks to the Moon, you will be more withdrawn and yet fizzing away below the surface in a way that only sensitive types can appreciate. Stand by for an explosion of emotion and passion in the days ahead.

22 SATURDAY
Moon Age Day 7 Moon Sign Scorpio

The going might be slightly tougher today, but it all depends on what you decide to undertake. Keep new incentives to a minimum and concentrate on one job at once. When the working day is over, be prepared to put your feet up. Even the resilient and frighteningly healthy Bull needs rest and relaxation from time to time.

23 SUNDAY
Moon Age Day 8 Moon Sign Sagittarius

This is one of the best times of the month for meeting interesting and influential people, but they won't drop out of the woodwork of their own accord. Seek out those you know can be particularly helpful and listen to what experts have to say about issues you haven't understood before. It's amazing what you can learn today.

24 MONDAY
Moon Age Day 9 Moon Sign Sagittarius

It will be very difficult for you to tolerate others telling you what to do at this time. Arguments are possible and if they do arise it is likely that they do so because you are less capable than usual of playing the game. Maybe that's not such a bad thing and it won't do too much harm to let the world know you have definite opinions.

25 TUESDAY   *Moon Age Day 10 Moon Sign Sagittarius*

This is one of the most favourable days of the month for affairs of the heart and for laying your feelings on the line. Finding the right words to express your emotions ought to be easier and you should be entirely truthful in your approach to romance. Your present attitude can be quite disarming in a number of different ways.

26 WEDNESDAY   *Moon Age Day 11 Moon Sign Capricorn*

Although you are still possessed of significant energy, you might find it slightly harder today to keep pace with new ideas. What isn't difficult is to understand how others feel and why they act in the way they do. You have great powers of persuasion and all you need to develop for overall success now is more self-confidence.

27 THURSDAY   *Moon Age Day 12 Moon Sign Capricorn*

Success at work comes quite naturally and this is a time during which you can gain a great deal as a result of the reservoir of good will you have built up over a long period of time. The time is right to influence people you know are on your side in any case. There are competitors about, but they are brushed aside.

28 FRIDAY   *Moon Age Day 13 Moon Sign Aquarius*

You should now be enjoying the practical world far more than would have been the case a week or two ago. New social prospects are also beckoning and you won't want to miss a moment of the excitement that seems to be at hand. Some of your victories at present will be short lived but you can still enjoy them whilst they last.

29 SATURDAY   *Moon Age Day 14 Moon Sign Aquarius*

Prepare for a significant boost to leisure and pleasure this weekend. In some ways you are slightly quieter inside yourself, but the world will do all it can to draw you out. Don't turn down any reasonable request for help, because there will be every chance for you to enjoy yourself whilst at the same time being extremely useful.

30 SUNDAY
Moon Age Day 15 Moon Sign Pisces

You can now get the maximum out of your family life and would also gain by discussing some of your deepest thoughts with a friend you trust absolutely. You still have plenty of energy and won't want to be left behind in the rush to get somewhere – or everywhere – today, but you might just be trying too hard for your own good.

31 MONDAY
Moon Age Day 16 Moon Sign Pisces

There is a tendency now for you to be so anxious to please people that you try to be everything to everyone. There comes a point when you simply have to do what seems right to you, even if it goes against the grain with people around you. Of course you will remain diplomatic, but you will still follow your own dictates.

September 2015

1 TUESDAY
Moon Age Day 17 Moon Sign Aries

A severe lack of progress is indicated and this can be put down to the position of the Moon in your solar twelfth house. This could stop you in your tracks as much as the lunar low can do, but you also have the ability to bluff your way through situations, if necessary. Everything will work out fine if you hang on to your sense of humour.

2 WEDNESDAY
Moon Age Day 18 Moon Sign Aries

Your thinking processes are now like lightning and you should definitely do all you can to make others listen to what you have to say. There is no point at all in being a shrinking violet because even if it seems at first that you have to bulldoze your ideas across, in the end most people will be very happy that you spoke out so pointedly.

3 THURSDAY
Moon Age Day 19 Moon Sign Taurus

Outward success is more or less assured, even if you may not always be entirely satisfied with what is going on inside your mind. Don't rule anything out for the moment, no matter how unlikely it might appear to be. Moving mountains is a difficult process but if anyone can do it, Taurus certainly can.

4 FRIDAY
Moon Age Day 20 Moon Sign Taurus

You can be especially confident right now that your ideas are as attractive to others as they are to you. You inspire so much confidence at the moment that practically everyone is willing to follow your lead. When it comes to romance, you have what it takes to knock someone for six – even if you have hesitated to try before.

5 SATURDAY
Moon Age Day 21 Moon Sign Gemini

Information arriving today could come from just about any direction and you need to be on the ball when it comes to getting things done. You have so much energy right now that even the most trying of tasks will be out of the way in a flash. Then when work is done, you will be happy to have fun!

6 SUNDAY
Moon Age Day 22 Moon Sign Gemini

Your mind works very quickly at the moment and you will be fully conversant with a whole host of possibilities while your friends are still jumping about from foot to foot. Others recognise your confident nature and will rely on you heavily for advice and practical assistance. Get to grips with a somewhat difficult personal issue.

7 MONDAY
Moon Age Day 23 Moon Sign Cancer

Keeping the right kind of company is favoured today and you can expect an interesting and stimulating sort of week ahead. Not everyone will be on your side at first, but you clearly have what it takes to talk people round and what is more you should be very diplomatic. Jobs will be out of the way in a flash.

8 TUESDAY
Moon Age Day 24 Moon Sign Cancer

Today you are more likely to find the greatest happiness at home, probably lost in a world of concepts and possibilities. There are all sorts of new facts coming in at the moment and that alone can prove to be the greatest fascination for you. Don't be too surprised if your partner does something that is quite out of character later.

9 WEDNESDAY
Moon Age Day 25 Moon Sign Cancer

Beneficial influences surround joint finances right now and you could do worse than to discuss the family budget with your partner or other family members. To some people this would be the bore of the week, but Taurus likes to have things sewn up and is never happier than when sorting out the future, especially where money is concerned.

10 THURSDAY
Moon Age Day 26 Moon Sign Leo

Along comes a time of significant energy and a determination on your part to take back command of situations over which you seem to have lost control. Be certain in the moves you make on the financial front. Once you have made up your mind about something, you need to stick to it, no matter what.

11 FRIDAY
Moon Age Day 27 Moon Sign Leo

Personal finances are likely to be on your mind today and you will want to do some organising in order to make sure there is going to be enough cash around at the end of this year. That probably means that you already have your eye on the Christmas period, perhaps because you have something very special planned this year.

12 SATURDAY
Moon Age Day 28 Moon Sign Virgo

It is really important today to make up your mind to follow a particular course of action and then to stick to it, even if those around you are inclined to disagree. It's a fact that you will be at odds with certain individuals at the moment, no matter what you do to try and put the situation right. You can thank the present position of Mars for this.

13 SUNDAY
Moon Age Day 0 Moon Sign Virgo

It looks as though you will continue to have great influence in the world you help to create and there is also potential excitement at hand. Not everyone is going to agree with either your point of view or your planned actions, but that doesn't really matter, because in the end you can bring them round in a very positive way.

14 MONDAY
Moon Age Day 1 Moon Sign Virgo

There are strong domestic impulses around right now. Although you might be rushed off your feet in the practical world, you will still find time to be kind and attentive to those you love the most. Don't allow yourself to be too tied to conventions of any sort and show how original you can be.

15 TUESDAY
Moon Age Day 2 Moon Sign Libra

The Moon now enters your solar twelfth house, which is going to slow things down a little and will at least give you the chance to regularise your life a little. You won't worry too much if you can't achieve everything you would wish, just as long as you know that most things are definitely going in the right direction.

16 WEDNESDAY
Moon Age Day 3 Moon Sign Libra

When it comes to communicating with others you should be very definitely in your element at the present time. There is very little happening that will put you out, even when surprises come thick and fast. A short journey of some sort could prove to be extremely interesting and might also bring a little more money your way.

17 THURSDAY
Moon Age Day 4 Moon Sign Scorpio

Take stock of your affairs today and by all means keep on planning, but don't get tied up in making arrangements to sign documents. On the social front, the lunar low might take the wind out of your sails, because it seems likely you will be far happier with your own company for the moment. This is no hardship to Taurus.

18 FRIDAY ☿
Moon Age Day 5 Moon Sign Scorpio

There might be a tendency for you to get caught up in one small problem after another today and it would be best all round if you left some of the worrying to others. You do more than your fair share as a rule, so it is only right that you let others take the strain now and again. Think up something really inspirational to do.

19 SATURDAY ☿
Moon Age Day 6 Moon Sign Scorpio

Added responsibilities might leave you feeling hard done by at this time. If so, be willing to share these around a little. Conflicts with authority figures are also possible, but much depends on your reactions and a low profile would probably be best. What you do need to maintain right now is your sense of purpose.

20 SUNDAY ☿ *Moon Age Day 7 Moon Sign Sagittarius*

Initiating social and romantic situations would be of interest to you today. The Sun remains in your solar fifth house and you should be very happy to be at the centre of whatever is taking place around you. Certain jobs could take longer to achieve than you anticipated, but you will get everything done all the same.

21 MONDAY ☿ *Moon Age Day 8 Moon Sign Sagittarius*

The time is right to pursue new educational interests and for study or travel. This is one of the best days of the month to look at new professional opportunities and at least some Taurus subjects will be mulling over a complete change in career. Almost anything that takes place around you can inspire your interest now.

22 TUESDAY ☿ *Moon Age Day 9 Moon Sign Capricorn*

Life should continue to be smooth and steady, though there could be a few instances when excitement rouses you to greater actions. In the main, you will be fairly happy to sit and watch for much of the time, only putting on an extra spurt when you know it is providential to do so. Aspects of love are also likely to be on your mind.

23 WEDNESDAY ☿ *Moon Age Day 10 Moon Sign Capricorn*

Progress at work should be flowing freely and this would seem to be a favourable day for signing contracts or beginning a new enterprise. You should be far more cheerful than you managed to be at the start of the week and can make more out of any small opportunity that is coming your way. Money matters should be easy to handle.

24 THURSDAY ☿ *Moon Age Day 11 Moon Sign Aquarius*

Teamwork can become important around now and you will be quite happy to throw in your lot with organisations you respect. It is fairly inevitable that when you do you will be expected to take a leading role and this might trouble you somewhat at first. You may seem to be on the move from morning until night today.

25 FRIDAY ☿ *Moon Age Day 12 Moon Sign Aquarius*

A boost to all practical and professional elements of your life comes along now that the Sun is in your solar sixth house. Progress across the next four weeks or so should be smoother and less erratic, which is likely to please you no end. You don't care for complications and always want to keep life running as smoothly as you can.

26 SATURDAY ☿ *Moon Age Day 13 Moon Sign Pisces*

Disagreements about everyday matters need to be avoided, especially since they cannot help to put matters right. Instead of niggling about situations, you need to wade in and sort them out once and for all. Rules and regulations are likely to get on your nerves at this time – unless, of course, you are the one who is making them.

27 SUNDAY ☿ *Moon Age Day 14 Moon Sign Pisces*

It looks as though the time is right for dealing with your public relations. The way others see you is very important and has a strong bearing on your future, so it is necessary to paint a good picture of yourself to the world at large. You can be trusted at the moment to present yourself in the best possible way to just about anyone.

28 MONDAY ☿ *Moon Age Day 15 Moon Sign Aries*

Try cultivating a greater awareness of the points of view that other people are putting across. It is even likely that closer attention to their opinions may have a profound bearing on your own medium-term thinking. Even someone who hasn't made a great degree of sense in the past is now more likely to impress you.

29 TUESDAY ☿ *Moon Age Day 16 Moon Sign Aries*

Developing new personality skills and making yourself generally useful to one and all will be high on your Tuesday agenda. The year is moving on rapidly and now would be as good a period as any to have a sort out at home, ahead of the winter months. At the same time, make use of any lingering good weather around now.

30 WEDNESDAY ☿   *Moon Age Day 17 Moon Sign Taurus*

Success is more or less assured under the influence of the lunar high and especially this time around, because the Sun is also so supportive in your solar chart. Today might have more to do with planning than actually taking action and you ought to find yourself with more time to have some fun.

October
2015

1 THURSDAY
☿ *Moon Age Day 18 Moon Sign Taurus*

This is definitely the right time to impress someone with your ideas and know-how. The lunar high makes you naturally dominant, very aspiring and good to know. Winning others round is no problem at all and you should discover that you have what it takes to be a real leader, even if you sometimes don't know where you are going!

2 FRIDAY
☿ *Moon Age Day 19 Moon Sign Gemini*

You are likely to be very opinionated at the moment and although that can be good in terms of getting your own way, it probably won't make you quite as popular as you can sometimes be. No matter what happens, it would be very sensible to retain a little diplomacy and to use some tact when dealing with important people.

3 SATURDAY
☿ *Moon Age Day 20 Moon Sign Gemini*

Now might be a good time to sort out your finances, maybe because your partner or family members are taking your advice in some way. You should also be enjoying a few indulgences under present trends and will be attracted to physical luxury. Try to make your home welcoming to acquaintances.

4 SUNDAY
☿ *Moon Age Day 21 Moon Sign Gemini*

With lots to keep you occupied, it looks as though today is going to be fast and furious. If anything, you will need more time to fit in everything you want to do. Much of what you undertake at the moment is likely to be away from the immediate environs of your home, though tomorrow will present a very different picture.

5 MONDAY ☿ *Moon Age Day 22 Moon Sign Cancer*

Although things are nowhere near as busy as they were a couple of days ago, you can relish the peace and quiet that has suddenly descended on you. For some it will be as if you are resting in the eye of a hurricane, because no matter how much is whizzing around you, very little of it seems to have a bearing on you personally.

6 TUESDAY ☿ *Moon Age Day 23 Moon Sign Cancer*

Any chance to broaden your horizons should be grasped with both hands as the pace of life gradually increases throughout today. Learning experiences will also be welcome, and no matter what your age it will be possible for you to make some stunning realisations. The adage 'you're never too old to learn' is especially true now.

7 WEDNESDAY ☿ *Moon Age Day 24 Moon Sign Leo*

Since you seem to be at some sort of mental peak right now your persuasive talents are present in great measure. You can put these to excellent use when it comes to business or family matters. Save some time for simple enjoyment and avoid getting so involved in paradoxes and conundrums that you fail to enjoy yourself.

8 THURSDAY ☿ *Moon Age Day 25 Moon Sign Leo*

This ought to be an especially productive period as far as your finances are concerned and you won't have any trouble at all getting others to follow your lead when it comes to monetary matters. You show yourself to be very wise and you are being careful and even frugal in your spending. Friends may be somewhat vague.

9 FRIDAY ☿ *Moon Age Day 26 Moon Sign Virgo*

Communication issues can be marred by a tendency towards arguments today, even if you are not the one who is causing the problems. Such situations only get in the way of the sort of progress you now want to make, which is why you will be very loath to get involved at all. If necessary, spend most of today working on your own.

10 SATURDAY ☿ *Moon Age Day 27 Moon Sign Virgo*

Although there are now likely to be unexpected demands placed upon you, the chances are that you will take the situation very much in your stride. You might have to be a little more patient with people who seem determined to frustrate your efforts, but you do have a great capacity at present to laugh and shrug your shoulders.

11 SUNDAY ☿ *Moon Age Day 28 Moon Sign Virgo*

You should now be able to capitalise well on social and communication matters. Look forward to plenty of activity, much of which is inspired by you in the first place. There might not be as much time for work as you would wish, but when it comes to enjoying yourself the sky is the limit.

12 MONDAY *Moon Age Day 29 Moon Sign Libra*

Although today should still be very enjoyable there could be a slight tendency for you to get carried away with your own big ideas. There is plenty of help around when you need it and probably also some timely advice. The problem is that Taurus doesn't always listen as much as it might and difficulties could be the result.

13 TUESDAY *Moon Age Day 0 Moon Sign Libra*

There can be some changes and alterations to take on board and this might mean having to react quickly to life, possibly in a way that makes you feel a little uncomfortable. Actually, it does you no harm at all to be put on the spot and if nothing else proves to you that you are more than capable of reacting to circumstances.

14 WEDNESDAY *Moon Age Day 1 Moon Sign Scorpio*

This would be the best possible time to manifest your personality and to be creative. Although you will probably be inclined to watch and wait in some situations you can make a sort of progress, though of the kind only an Earth sign such as Taurus would fully understand. Clubs and societies may hold a fascination for you now.

15 THURSDAY *Moon Age Day 2 Moon Sign Scorpio*

Certain plans could receive something of a setback and you have to acknowledge the presence of the lunar low, even if you would rather just push on as normal. You might feel a definite urge to indulge yourself in some way and since other planetary trends show you being especially close to family members, your home really counts now.

16 FRIDAY *Moon Age Day 3 Moon Sign Scorpio*

The accent is now on romance and fun, which might not leave all that much time for you to concentrate on issues that are stacking up in the wings. Don't be in the least surprised that you're not worried about something that would normally trouble you no end. You act on impulse at the moment.

17 SATURDAY *Moon Age Day 4 Moon Sign Sagittarius*

Your charitable instincts are very strong at the moment, but this doesn't mean you should be throwing your money away on a whim. This is unlike you, of course, and you should be able to help those around you without adversely affecting your own future prospects and bank balance.

18 SUNDAY *Moon Age Day 5 Moon Sign Sagittarius*

It would seem that the further you manage to go in terms of travel, the better this period is likely to be. Of course, it is quite likely that you will find it impossible to go anywhere at the moment. This doesn't mean that all is lost, because you have a tremendous capacity for journeying in your head – which is better than nothing.

19 MONDAY *Moon Age Day 6 Moon Sign Capricorn*

Work and practical matters can be tiresome on occasion. This is why you will be leaving others to do some of the donkeywork, whilst you look at things and plan carefully. Not that there is likely to be any lack of energy on your part. On the contrary, you can party all night long if necessary, but only if you want to.

20 TUESDAY

Moon Age Day 7 Moon Sign Capricorn

Business matters suddenly look good, but it really depends on your tenacity and your common sense. You have both of these in great proportion, so it appears that this ought to be an ideal week for you. If there is a fly in the ointment at this time it could be your inability to come to terms with the plans of colleagues as the days unfold.

21 WEDNESDAY

Moon Age Day 8 Moon Sign Capricorn

There is a chance that you will get drawn into other people's personal conflicts, which is not a good idea. Try to stay on the outside of disputes, but if you find you have no choice but to become involved, make sure you win the day quickly and efficiently.

22 THURSDAY

Moon Age Day 9 Moon Sign Aquarius

Friendships should prove to be very rewarding under present trends and you are likely to turn to your pals time and again today. This would be an excellent day for entertaining others and for showing just how smart and well organised your house is. If this is not the case, it's time to start moving things around.

23 FRIDAY

Moon Age Day 10 Moon Sign Aquarius

You need to build up to maximum efficiency at work and to make sure that everything is sorted out to your satisfaction ahead of the weekend. This means you will begin next week in a tidy and efficient manner. It ought to be possible to pull a few strings today, because you are in the good books of those who have influence.

24 SATURDAY

Moon Age Day 11 Moon Sign Pisces

You express charm, grace and harmony at the moment, all of which makes you popular with others and happy with yourself. Confidence should be growing in your professional life and it isn't out of the question that you will be taking on some new responsibilities, probably as a result of someone else experiencing a failure.

25 SUNDAY
Moon Age Day 12 Moon Sign Pisces

With your love life in potentially good shape, your powers of attraction have rarely been better. To some Bulls it might almost seem as though you are too popular, which is, at least, an enviable position to be in. All the same, it is possible that the present situation could cause a little jealousy amongst your admirers.

26 MONDAY
Moon Age Day 13 Moon Sign Aries

Prepare to make the most of friendships today and throughout the week. Things are going to slow down for a day or two, which is why you need to focus all your energy in specific directions today. The evening should be left free for socialising and for mixing with people you find fascinating.

27 TUESDAY
Moon Age Day 14 Moon Sign Aries

Take it easy at home and save your energy for another day. The best possible scenario today represents you being surrounded by people who think you are wonderful. You can move easily from one enjoyable situation to another. Don't throw a spanner in the works by being anxious and fussy.

28 WEDNESDAY
Moon Age Day 15 Moon Sign Taurus

Your main area of fulfilment comes from relationships of many different sorts and whilst the lunar high is around you continue to seek out interesting people and situations. It is also likely that your curiosity will be aroused and this will make you look deeper into certain situations than would often be the case.

29 THURSDAY
Moon Age Day 16 Moon Sign Taurus

You now have a strong personal magnetism that is inspiring to the people you contact in your daily life. They will find you interesting to be around and will want to engage you in conversation. It is not out of the question that someone will invite you to take part in what is likely to be a significant and very enjoyable adventure.

30 FRIDAY
Moon Age Day 17 Moon Sign Gemini

Be ready to make compromises today and don't be too keen to have your own way in every situation. The more flexible you are, the greater is the chance that Lady Luck will smile on you. The Bull is not generally a gambler, but there are a few chances that might be worth taking today and the results will probably surprise even you.

31 SATURDAY
Moon Age Day 18 Moon Sign Gemini

You may now need to get rid of something in order to make life less emotionally complicated. Taurus is thinking very deeply about personal issues and there is a chance that you will be analysing things too much. A light and bright approach would work best, so try not to take anything more seriously than you have to.

♉ November 2015

1 SUNDAY
Moon Age Day 19 Moon Sign Cancer

Not everyone is going to appreciate the fact that you are speaking your mind today and if there are any difficulties regarding your outspoken manner, these are likely to be at home. Things are going to be very different in other spheres of your life, because from a social point of view everyone you meet is interested in your opinions.

2 MONDAY
Moon Age Day 20 Moon Sign Cancer

It could be that you are putting across your point of view a little forcefully early this week and in all honesty you would get on better if you relaxed more. Hang fire with certain projects and ideas whilst you get existing jobs out of the way. If you don't crowd your schedule, you will remain more relaxed and better to know.

3 TUESDAY
Moon Age Day 21 Moon Sign Leo

Things could be somewhat tenuous as far as finances are concerned. It's not that anything is likely to be going wrong; more that you don't recognise the sort of momentum regarding money that makes Taurus happy. On the personal front, you have what it takes at the moment to bring extra zip into your romantic life.

4 WEDNESDAY
Moon Age Day 22 Moon Sign Leo

You will certainly have your work cut out in personal attachments today, though in the main you will be far more cheerful and reactive than has been the case for a day or two. You have some excellent advice to give others and most of this comes from the reservoir of experience you have accumulated throughout the years.

5 THURSDAY
Moon Age Day 23 Moon Sign Leo

It looks as though you will be extremely generous today and this is more than a case of throwing a pound or two into the nearest charity tin. On the contrary, you will put yourself out significantly in order to help people you recognise as being in emotional pain or distress. You can even be of help in some ways that you will never realise.

6 FRIDAY
Moon Age Day 24 Moon Sign Virgo

Professional developments could seem to be rather hard going and for that reason you might have to rely more on the help and advice of colleagues. This won't go down especially well if you have been in open competition with one or two of them, but despite yourself you could make a new friend as a result of your present needs.

7 SATURDAY
Moon Age Day 25 Moon Sign Virgo

Right now there are likely to be some very pleasurable encounters taking place and this is definitely a Saturday during which you need to take time out for personal enjoyment. Who knows what awaits you out there in the big, wide world? It's a case of being present to recognise the possibilities, so get out of bed early and take part.

8 SUNDAY
Moon Age Day 26 Moon Sign Libra

This is a good day during which to be in the social mainstream and you should get a wonderful response from almost anyone you come across. Not that you are leaving anything to chance at the moment. On the contrary, you are filled with a desire to check and double-check all details, which is great for you but could annoy someone.

9 MONDAY
Moon Age Day 27 Moon Sign Libra

New initiatives in the romantic department for some Taurus subjects could lead to a very interesting and maybe even a fairly surprising Monday. If you have been looking for a new relationship, this is one of the times of the year to keep your eyes open. First dates should work out well, but established attachments are good, too.

10 TUESDAY　　　*Moon Age Day 28　Moon Sign Libra*

Romantic affairs are now even more positively highlighted, and the accent is definitely on 'affairs' in the case of some Taurus subjects. Try as best you can to keep your attachments out in the open, because clandestine meetings are likely to leave you feeling guilty and dishonest. Find friends in whom you can confide.

11 WEDNESDAY　　　*Moon Age Day 29　Moon Sign Scorpio*

With the lunar low comes what might turn out to be the quietest and least eventful time you will experience during November. If you can't make any headway, then you might as well take a break. A few tasks that probably seemed necessary yesterday now take their place at the back of your mind and are not really urgent at all.

12 THURSDAY　　　*Moon Age Day 0　Moon Sign Scorpio*

This remains a good time for doing as little as possible in a physical sense. This is not to suggest that you will stagnate in any way. On the contrary, your mind remains very active and your capacity for prior planning has rarely been better than it is right now. Instead of bemoaning the presence of the lunar low, you can use it effectively.

13 FRIDAY　　　*Moon Age Day 1　Moon Sign Sagittarius*

It looks as though you are now in for a period of great nostalgia, which is not unusual as the nights become longer and winter really takes hold. Stick to your favourite people for now, though this doesn't mean locking yourself into your own castle. Friends could prove to be just as important to you now as family members.

14 SATURDAY　　　*Moon Age Day 2　Moon Sign Sagittarius*

You seem to be very tuned in to the emotional state of those with whom you interact today. This will be especially true in the case of your partner or loved ones but is also somewhat the case in more casual relationships. Because you are so sensitive, people are more likely to recognise the fact and to single you out for their confessions.

15 SUNDAY   *Moon Age Day 3 Moon Sign Sagittarius*

Some matters will be a little off course, though you still won't have the necessary energy to wade into life with your usual appetite. On the contrary, you are likely to leave quite a few things to colleagues and friends, whilst you adopt a sort of dreamy attitude. This is quite natural and even crucial for Taurus from time to time.

16 MONDAY   *Moon Age Day 4 Moon Sign Capricorn*

Your desire to make everyone else happy is laudable, but it might also be somewhat idealistic. The saying goes that you can't please all the people all of the time and you are about to discover how true this is. Stay flexible and continue to assist when you can, but you also have to realise that some people will never be content.

17 TUESDAY   *Moon Age Day 5 Moon Sign Capricorn*

Your flair for detail is noteworthy and it appears that you know exactly how to make things look and feel right in your immediate vicinity. What you probably can't do at the moment is to make everyone around you as happy as you seem to be. That will prove to be a frustration, because Taurus wants the universe to be perfect.

18 WEDNESDAY   *Moon Age Day 6 Moon Sign Aquarius*

This is a time to widen your horizons and become very expansive in your thinking. If you turn your attention towards personal finances today you can probably think up ways to make more money. This might be by streamlining situations and taking a new look at old and outdated ways of behaving.

19 THURSDAY   *Moon Age Day 7 Moon Sign Aquarius*

Although short-term success is not very likely right now, you do have good notions that can be put to the test in the days and weeks ahead. It may appear that something you really want is being denied, but that won't be the way things turn out. Later in the day you should be monitoring a few pleasant surprises coming from friends.

20 FRIDAY   *Moon Age Day 8 Moon Sign Pisces*

It is generally easy for you to be tolerant and understanding, which is probably just as well on this particular Friday. Relatives could drive you up the wall with their requests, but you will still manage to smile and to be your usual courteous self. This should be a good time for business transactions and also for making new friends.

21 SATURDAY   *Moon Age Day 9 Moon Sign Pisces*

Although this may not turn out to be the most productive weekend you have ever known, it does have its own significant advantages. For one thing, you will realise just how much affection surrounds you, which can be very heart-warming. This would be a good time to get together with family members to discuss events later in the year.

22 SUNDAY   *Moon Age Day 10 Moon Sign Aries*

Emotional challenges that appear around now are like the morning mist and will probably disappear almost as soon as they arrive. You could be slightly more inclined towards worry, but most of your anxiety will be theoretical and without good cause. Try to relax and let other people spoil you. In particular, don't fret about money.

23 MONDAY   *Moon Age Day 11 Moon Sign Aries*

Though work relationships tend to be steady at this time, people you deal with in a more personal sense could seem touchy and difficult to deal with. Part of the problem is likely to be your own approach, because you won't have the level of understanding or tolerance that is usually the case. Avoid getting tied up with pointless details.

24 TUESDAY   *Moon Age Day 12 Moon Sign Taurus*

Personal matters are now positively spotlighted and it looks as though you can expect a wealth of compliments to be coming your way. Put this together with all the attention that is being paid to you and it becomes obvious that the lunar high is really doing you some favours this month. Finances should be stronger now.

25 WEDNESDAY   *Moon Age Day 13 Moon Sign Taurus*

This is a time during which you ought to be putting more faith in Lady Luck. This doesn't mean putting your shirt on the next horse running, but it is a favourable time for throwing in your lot with fortune in non-financial ways. A better attitude becomes possible when you are dealing with an old and rather difficult family issue.

26 THURSDAY   *Moon Age Day 14 Moon Sign Gemini*

If you can learn the necessary balance between past situations and what faces you now, you can make great progress in your life as a whole. You can expect solid and steady growth throughout what is left of November and will be quite willing to put new ideas to people who may well be in a position to offer you their support.

27 FRIDAY   *Moon Age Day 15 Moon Sign Gemini*

Events could suddenly arise that cause you to think again about some of your friendships. Be careful, because gossip is not the same as proof. As you usually do, it is necessary to give anyone the benefit of the doubt until you can be sure of what is taking place. Make sure you don't worry about things you can't alter.

28 SATURDAY   *Moon Age Day 16 Moon Sign Cancer*

Unpredictable things can happen at this time and you need to be able to react quickly to changing circumstances. As a result, your usual equilibrium could be shaken somewhat, but it does you good to be forced into different modes of thinking on occasion. It is likely that family members will support you in your plans.

29 SUNDAY   *Moon Age Day 17 Moon Sign Cancer*

Gather all your reserves of willpower and wherever possible stick to what you know to be right, even if the whole world disagrees with you. There are times when your mixture of intuition and practical common sense are worth more than gold. Today is one of those occasions and you need to have the courage of your convictions.

30 MONDAY

Moon Age Day 18 Moon Sign Cancer

This may be a fruitful day for those who are looking for new love. Social trends are good, so prepare to meet people you find truly inspiring. Not everyone is equally trustworthy, so before you embark upon something completely new and revolutionary you need to double-check facts with those you know are reliable.

⑧ December 2015

1 TUESDAY
Moon Age Day 19 Moon Sign Leo

This is a day during which priorities on the domestic front might prevent you from working as hard in other ways as you might wish. Any gains that come along tend to be quick and you will have to be equally speedy in order to make the most of them. What you might enjoy more than anything today is a good chat with friends.

2 WEDNESDAY
Moon Age Day 20 Moon Sign Leo

A very romantic and light-hearted period comes along and you are unlikely to take anything all that seriously for the next couple of days at least. Your humorous attitude to life will be appreciated by most of those around you, but maybe not by everyone. Leave grumpy sorts alone and look around for people who want to laugh with you.

3 THURSDAY
Moon Age Day 21 Moon Sign Virgo

You can now see all too well how important feelings are to your present life and your hopes for the future. You should be right on the ball when it comes to manoeuvring others into the right position and your persuasive powers are likely to be extremely good. What you could lack is the level of general good luck you need.

4 FRIDAY
Moon Age Day 22 Moon Sign Virgo

Your cheery mood today could prove to be quite infectious and comes as a great alteration after the last few days. There are gains to be made through pushing your luck more than you usually might and you have what it takes to turn heads in both work and social situations. You look especially attractive to others now.

5 SATURDAY
Moon Age Day 23 Moon Sign Libra

You could be in a restless frame of mind, but your optimism can be quite infectious. Some Taurus subjects will already have Christmas in view and it is likely that your social life is increasing in intensity. People will be more open to your opinions and will actively seek you out to offer the sort of advice for which Taurus is famous.

6 SUNDAY
Moon Age Day 24 Moon Sign Libra

You now combine energy and courage with ambition and self-control. It's a formidable recipe and the result is likely to be appealing to everyone. Defending others will come as second nature today and you won't hold back, whether your opinions are being sought or not. Try to be at least moderate in your advice.

7 MONDAY
Moon Age Day 25 Moon Sign Libra

Family relationships should be a wonderful thing at the moment and the Christmas spirit is almost certainly prevailing in your household well ahead of the actual festivities. You should be getting on especially well with younger members of the family, but you are likely to reserve your most intense warmth for your lover.

8 TUESDAY
Moon Age Day 26 Moon Sign Scorpio

You would be much better off today keeping a low profile and attending to your own needs without getting too involved in the world at large. Whilst the lunar low is around, you will be quieter and less inclined to involve yourself in group or social activities. You will be fairly happy to find your own chair by the fireside.

9 WEDNESDAY
Moon Age Day 27 Moon Sign Scorpio

Some of your desire to please others is likely to fail for the moment, which may incline you to stop trying. This would be a mistake, because in a day or two everything is likely to look very different. Even by the end of today, you will probably be feeling better about yourself and you may even be willing to go out and have fun.

10 THURSDAY   *Moon Age Day 28 Moon Sign Sagittarius*

This is a favourable time for social and romantic situations and you are a real winner when in company under present planetary trends. Any hope of making significant progress at work is probably now out of the window, because there is too much else going on. The attitude of a close friend could be difficult to understand and impossible to alter.

11 FRIDAY   *Moon Age Day 0 Moon Sign Sagittarius*

The best way to get your own way right now is to act indirectly and to use a little psychology when you are dealing with complicated people. It won't be easy to understand everyone, but then it probably isn't necessary either. Cut through red tape at work and get to where you need to be as quickly as proves to be possible.

12 SATURDAY   *Moon Age Day 1 Moon Sign Sagittarius*

Beware of emotional drives that could lead you to doing things you would never normally consider. They could also bring you to being argumentative, even with people who clearly have your best interests at heart. Avoid being prickly and if you can discuss things without losing your temper, so much the better.

13 SUNDAY   *Moon Age Day 2 Moon Sign Capricorn*

Family issues remain pressing and you seem to be jumping around from foot to foot for the moment: half committed to sorting things out at home, but equally keen to get on with practicalities far from your own front door. Even Taurus can't achieve everything, so it will be important to prioritise and to do first things first.

14 MONDAY   *Moon Age Day 3 Moon Sign Capricorn*

Your routines can be altered, not only by Christmas, but also by small but irritating mishaps. You need to be especially careful at present and should not take undue risks, especially with fragile objects. Nevertheless there is much good humour about for the moment, plus the chance to cuddle up with the person you love most.

15 TUESDAY   *Moon Age Day 4 Moon Sign Aquarius*

This is an excellent period for having major insights and for coming to conclusions quickly and without much forethought. Being so efficient there is little that seems to be beyond your capabilities and you will charge through many jobs in half the usual time. This would also be a good day to persuade people to follow your lead.

16 WEDNESDAY   *Moon Age Day 5 Moon Sign Aquarius*

Perhaps your loved ones will now have some difficulty realising how deep your emotions are running and it may be necessary to let some of them in on your deepest feelings. This probably won't be easy because although you are always warm and open, when it comes to your inner feelings you can be a closed book.

17 THURSDAY   *Moon Age Day 6 Moon Sign Pisces*

This is definitely a time to get rid of sentimentality, because you are after the stark truth of situations whilst the Sun is in your solar eighth house. This is always the time of year for practical action in the Taurus life and you will also be bearing in mind that Christmas is just around the corner. Your social life should be on the up.

18 FRIDAY   *Moon Age Day 7 Moon Sign Pisces*

You arrive at the middle of a dynamic and inspiring period. Your restlessness and the desire for change are paramount, all of which can make you inclined to fidget more than usual. The one thing you will find almost impossible to do will be to settle for the mundane. The more excitement that comes along the better you feel.

19 SATURDAY   *Moon Age Day 8 Moon Sign Aries*

There may be opportunities for favourable partnerships at the moment and you tend to be just about as outgoing as Taurus ever gets. People will naturally rely on you for advice and you seem to have a bottomless reservoir of ideas. It's a pity you cannot organise yourself as well as you can organise others around this time.

20 SUNDAY
Moon Age Day 9 Moon Sign Aries

You must eliminate old ideas and take a long, hard look at your motivations whilst the planets are in their present positions. There is time enough to get rid of anything that is old or outdated, and you are clearly in the right frame of mind to stretch yourself still further. There won't be as much time as you would wish for family matters.

21 MONDAY
Moon Age Day 10 Moon Sign Aries

You remain fairly impulsive and might do a few things that are not all that well thought out. Nevertheless, you have the capacity to keep going and to get yourself out of a tight corner if it proves to be necessary. Get that last-minute shopping out of the way today if you can.

22 TUESDAY
Moon Age Day 11 Moon Sign Taurus

Don't avoid necessary change today, but learn to embrace it instead. Almost everything that happens can be turned to your advantage and you show yourself to the world in the best possible light. Few will doubt your sincerity or your capacity for hard work. Everything ought to come together to offer you a potentially sensational time.

23 WEDNESDAY
Moon Age Day 12 Moon Sign Taurus

Now the Moon is firmly in your own zodiac sign and the lunar high for December is likely to be a fast and furious period. Your level of energy is high and there is extra motivation coming from your work and from all practical matters in your life. Play on your tendency to be lucky at the moment and take the odd small risk.

24 THURSDAY
Moon Age Day 13 Moon Sign Gemini

You should be on top form for Christmas Eve and you are very likely to enjoy a day that is split right down the middle in terms of enjoyment and work. Nothing is too much trouble when you are dealing with your family and especially your partner. Look out for a real, nostalgic romantic interlude in the evening.

153

25 FRIDAY
Moon Age Day 14 Moon Sign Gemini

You show yourself as being a larger than life character and that means an even greater increase in your general popularity. Last-minute invitations are likely to be coming from many different directions and you will be doing all you can to accommodate your fan club. You can create your own sunshine on Christmas Day, no matter what the weather is actually doing.

26 SATURDAY
Moon Age Day 15 Moon Sign Cancer

It is possible you will feel the urge to provoke others into thinking more deeply about issues that have been shelved for quite some time. A certain impatience still attends many of your actions and you haven't altered much in your present desire to make things happen. There might be time later in the day to get some genuine rest, but not much.

27 SUNDAY
Moon Age Day 16 Moon Sign Cancer

Some alterations in your routines should be enough to keep you focused and motivated, but what you shouldn't do at the moment is make yourself a slave to convention. There is a certain sense of security for Taurus in always doing the same thing in the same way, but for now at least you need to alter your routines deliberately.

28 MONDAY
Moon Age Day 17 Moon Sign Leo

Your mind is inspired, and although there will be plenty to get done in a practical sense, this is not the sphere of life that will interest you the most. On the contrary, you want to mix and mingle all the time and will do everything you can in order to merge the practical side of life with your burning desire to join in.

29 TUESDAY
Moon Age Day 18 Moon Sign Leo

It might seem as if you are possessed by a restless spirit and a need to know everything that is going on around you. It's true that things may begin to slow during the second half of the day, but for most of this Tuesday you are still running at top speed. Don't be at all surprised if you wear yourself out physically.

30 WEDNESDAY   *Moon Age Day 19 Moon Sign Virgo*

The urge to see new places and to have different experiences is strong, though you will also be settling down somewhat in your own mind. You have the ability to express yourself very well and you leave those around you in no doubt that you know what you are doing. Doubts are for others now and certainly not for you.

31 THURSDAY   *Moon Age Day 20 Moon Sign Virgo*

There is now the chance of increased freedom that you can use for greater creativity and better self-expression. There could be a tendency for you to be quite bossy but those who know you well are aware of how to deal with this. Create party fun tonight and make sure everyone joins in.

RISING SIGNS FOR TAURUS

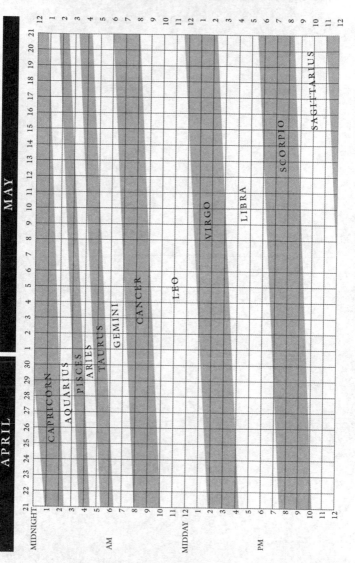

THE ZODIAC, PLANETS AND CORRESPONDENCES

The Earth revolves around the Sun once every calendar year, so when viewed from Earth the Sun appears in a different part of the sky as the year progresses. In astrology, these parts of the sky are divided into the signs of the zodiac and this means that the signs are organised in a circle. The circle begins with Aries and ends with Pisces.

Taking the zodiac sign as a starting point, astrologers then work with all the positions of planets, stars and many other factors to calculate horoscopes and birth charts and tell us what the stars have in store for us.

The table below shows the planets and Elements for each of the signs of the zodiac. Each sign belongs to one of the four Elements: Fire, Air, Earth or Water. Fire signs are creative and enthusiastic; Air signs are mentally active and thoughtful; Earth signs are constructive and practical; Water signs are emotional and have strong feelings.

It also shows the metals and gemstones associated with, or corresponding with, each sign. The correspondence is made when a metal or stone possesses properties that are held in common with a particular sign of the zodiac.

Finally, the table shows the opposite of each star sign – this is the opposite sign in the astrological circle.

Placed	Sign	Symbol	Element	Planet	Metal	Stone	Opposite
1	Aries	Ram	Fire	Mars	Iron	Bloodstone	Libra
2	Taurus	Bull	Earth	Venus	Copper	Sapphire	Scorpio
3	Gemini	Twins	Air	Mercury	Mercury	Tiger's Eye	Sagittarius
4	Cancer	Crab	Water	Moon	Silver	Pearl	Capricorn
5	Leo	Lion	Fire	Sun	Gold	Ruby	Aquarius
6	Virgo	Maiden	Earth	Mercury	Mercury	Sardonyx	Pisces
7	Libra	Scales	Air	Venus	Copper	Sapphire	Aries
8	Scorpio	Scorpion	Water	Pluto	Plutonium	Jasper	Taurus
9	Sagittarius	Archer	Fire	Jupiter	Tin	Topaz	Gemini
10	Capricorn	Goat	Earth	Saturn	Lead	Black Onyx	Cancer
11	Aquarius	Waterbearer	Air	Uranus	Uranium	Amethyst	Leo
12	Pisces	Fishes	Water	Neptune	Tin	Moonstone	Virgo